Received on

FEB 0 8 2018

More Advance Praise
for *Baker's Royale*, by Naomi Robinson:

In *Baker's Royale*, Naomi Robinson puts the most magical
and modern spin on dessert classics we all know and love.
This is a book I will use time and time again.

—JOCELYN DELK ADAMS, author of *Grandbaby Cakes*

Naomi Robinson is the queen of the drizzle, dollop, and swirl! Her
desserts are guaranteed to make you look like a baking rock star!
—GABY DALKIN, of What's Gaby Cooking

Naomi's blog has always been my go-to for the most indulgent,
beautiful desserts. She creates one-of-a-kind masterpieces
that I can actually make at home!

—JESSICA MERCHANT, author of *Seriously Delish*

Baker's Royale

75 *Twists* on
All Your Favorite Sweets

→ ⁝ **NAOMI ROBINSON** ⁝ ←

Running Press
PHILADELPHIA

Running Press
Hachette Book Group
1290 Avenue of the Americas, New York, NY 10104
www.runningpress.com
@Running_Press

Printed in China

First Edition: September 2017

Published by Running Press, an imprint of Perseus Books, LLC,
a subsidiary of Hachette Book Group, Inc.

The Hachette Speakers Bureau provides a wide range of authors for speaking events. To find out more, go to www.hachettespeakersbureau.com or call (866) 376-6591.

The publisher is not responsible for websites (or their content) that are not owned by the publisher.

Photographs Copyright © 2017 by Kristin Teig, except where noted

Photographs on pages 25, 28, 50-51, 53, 68, 81, 87, 109-111, 113, 126, 148, 158, 183, 186, 189, 195, 211, 216, 218-219, 221, 224, 237, 245, 248, 253, 256 Copyright © 2017 by Naomi Robinson

Print book cover and interior design by Ashley Todd

Library of Congress Control Number: 2017939299

ISBNs: 978-0-7624-5928-5 (hardcover), 978-0-7624-6114-1 (ebook)

L. Rex

10 9 8 7 6 5 4 3 2 1

To Matt and the boys —
the only sweets
a girl really needs.

Contents

Acknowledgments

THIS BOOK WAS the ultimate labor of love, one that would not have been possible if it weren't for the support of so many awesome people!

To Lisa Grubka and Kristen Green Wiewora, who believed in me and the recipes and saw it through from the beginning to the end. Thank you for the many coaching calls that were taken between carpool shuffling, crying babies, and late-night conversations once the kids were asleep. I'm humbled and grateful you were both there to help me cross the finish line.

To Ashley Todd and the Running Press team, who brought beauty to chaos. You gave my vision a home on these printed pages.

To Rachel Holtzman, for being the sounding board and finesse to my nonlinear thoughts and words.

To Billy Green for helping me keep my sanity through the whole process. I could not ask for a better partner in the kitchen.

To the readers of BakersRoyale.com, who bake and laugh along with me on a weekly basis. This book is our book. We now have another place to meet, to eat, to drink, and have fun in the kitchen together.

To Teri Olson, for being a constant and continued source of inspiration, strength, and reassurance. But most of all, your kindness and generosity in life has taught me more than you know.

To my wild bunch: Blake for your brutal honesty as a taste tester (even when you didn't know you were being one); Cole, my little mad chef and kitchen assistant, for all your mash-up inspiration and suggestions; Connor, my little cookie stealer, for bringing your chubby toddler cheeks and laughter into the kitchen when it got too serious.

And most important, to my husband, Matt, for his unwavering support and belief in me. This book could not have happened without you. As with every adventure we start, your ability to make me laugh when I need it the most continues to carry me through our adventures in and out of the kitchen. Everything leads back to you. I love you.

Introduction

I'VE NEVER BEEN a linear person in most aspects of my life. I like the twisting roads, the blind spots, the detours—it's where all the magical mistakes happen. It's through these unforeseen turns that sinkhole cakes turn into leveled beauties, imploding macarons become smooth and elegant, and weepy meringues transform into fluffy, chewy clouds. It's where you discover that cookie batter makes for the perfect, crisp foundation of a bark, that bright citrus has an elegant side with an infusion of Earl Grey tea, and that croissants—when soaked in a cinnamon-espresso custard—take bread pudding to a whole new level. For this self taught baker, trial and error, experimentation, and jumping into the deep end with eyes squeezed shut have yielded some of the best treats and confections I could never have dreamed up on my own.

But I didn't always know that a winding path would lead me to the perfect job, too. Before I started baking—and writing about it—as a career, I was working in an office. I'd sit in meetings with frosting-smeared pants, working out in my head why a recipe was failing or how to get it to that next level of delicious. Instead of fielding e-mails and meeting deadlines, I was answering reader mail on my newly minted blog, BakersRoyale.com.

At home, it wasn't much better. Home-cooked meals turned into my trying to peddle cupcakes to my (gasp) cake-loathing son while we waited for my husband to come home with take-out. I ran the mixer past midnight. Self-maintenance slipped until I was washing my hair every third day (okay, more like every fourth day). I was trying to live a double—heck, triple—life: mom, office drone, and aspiring professional baking blogger. It wasn't long before the day came where I had to make a choice: keep up the status quo, or believe that all the sugar and butter I was creaming in every free minute was the answer to a calmer, more satisfying life.

I made the right choice.

I traded in Excel spreadsheets for kitchen tools and gained a community of home bakers who, regardless of their skill level, were baking along with me. They cheered me on, supported me when I felt like giving up, gave me invaluable feedback, and best of all, helped make me a better baker.

And that is exactly what this book is about: becoming a better baker. For the recipes in this book—just as on my blog—skill level carries no consequence. It doesn't matter whether you've been wielding your whisk for a month or a lifetime (or had to order one online just now to get started). Never mind if you've never worked with gelatin or if you don't know your tarts from your truffles. There is no prescribed program for becoming a "good" baker, no progression of recipes that leads to the perfect cake, no linear path. All mistakes are learning opportunities, and because it's baking, they tend to be just as delicious as the victories—if a little messier. Keep this in mind as you work your way through the desserts in this book: The success of the recipes is a foregone conclusion that only time and willingness dictates. You will eventually get to fluffy-as-a-dream frosting and perfectly coiffed candies. And whatever you do, don't be afraid of imperfection. Serve your layered cake even if it's not perfectly level! Arrange those misshapen bars on a platter as though you were serving the most beautiful dessert! Believe me, no one has ever told me, "Gosh, I'm not going to taste that less than perfect éclair."

Just get organized—seriously, you don't want to be shuffling around looking for pots, pans, and ingredients while you're trying to bake cupcakes—and get in the kitchen. I promise these recipes are going to get you there.

These recipes, after all, are just as big a part of my journey as baking in the

first place. Five years ago, uninspired by baking the same old recipes, I began creating updated versions of the classics. Ho-hum cheesecake got a fluffy ricotta-based, lemon-scented facelift. Outdated spumoni got spun into a fresh and fun ice cream cake. The only criteria I used were: Is it delicious? Can it be for the everyday *and* the extraordinary? And will it look as if I spent all day working when, in fact, it really was a snap? Check, check, and check.

The desserts in this book are a fusion of refined classics and everyday indulgence: classic southern Chess Pie made über-decadent with brown butter and chocolate; the simple cupcake gone carnival with the addition of crispy funnel cake toppers; and truffles given an unexpected twist with the natural combo of beer and pretzels. Want to get fancy and create a crowd-pleaser without buying thirty ingredients and a $400 mixer? Then go for the Caramel, Pear, and Walnut Cake with Crème Fraîche Whipped Cream. Feeling nostalgic? Your childhood favorites now have just enough refinement to also feel grown-up, such as Graham Dutch Apple Pie and Cannoli Cakelets. You'll find that simple flavor pairings can turn ordinary ingredients into the most sophisticated upgrade, such as London Fog Blueberry Hand Pies and Apricot Coconut Bars. Need a morning kick-starter that will actually make you look forward to the alarm? Try Campfire Granola Bars or Mini Cinnamon Rolls. And let's not forget about such tried-and-true crowd-pleasers (and bake sale must-haves) as Caramel Popcorn Cookies and Chocolate Mousse Fudge Brownies. From small treats to belt-busters, get ready to have your candy, cake, and cookies and eat them, too.

COOKIES, BROWNIES, AND BARS

few of my favorite things, to be sure. I love how easy they are to put together, and they never fail to scratch the comfort food itch. And because they're typically built on a very simple foundation (butter, sugar, eggs, flour, mix), playing around with these classic recipes is how I initially learned how to riff. No one's disappointed when such treats as Rocky Road Cookies, Campfire Granola Bars, or Speculoos Brownie Cake show up at a birthday party or bake sale.

CARAMEL-FTILED CHOCOLATE CRINKLE COOKIES

I'm notorious for having a heavy hand when it comes dessert—I mean, why just make cookies when you can stuff them with caramel-filled chocolates?! This was one of my first forays into the world of candy-filled cookies, but I was hooked after the first batch. They're delightfully ooey-gooey and offer a starting point of crazy variations with no end, like stuffing your favorite cookie inside or other bite-size candy pieces (though this one's my favorite by far). My boys call them "dunkers" because there is so much dunking going on that by the end of the cookie eating session, their milk has practically become chocolate cookie-flavored milk!

MAKES 18 TO 20 COOKIES

1   cup (120 g) all-purpose flour

1   teaspoon baking powder

½   teaspoon instant espresso powder

¼   teaspoon salt

6   tablespoons (86 g) unsalted butter

⅔   cup (60 g) unsweetened cocoa powder, sifted

1½ cups (300 g) light brown sugar

2   large eggs, at room temperature

18 to 20 Rolos candies (one per cookie)

½   cup (59 g) confectioners' sugar, sifted

Directions

Preheat the oven to 350°F (180°C). Line 2 baking sheets with parchment paper and set aside.

In a medium bowl, whisk together the flour, baking powder, espresso powder, and salt. Set aside.

In a medium saucepan over medium heat, melt the butter. Remove from the heat and stir in the cocoa powder and brown sugar. Add the eggs, 1 at a time, whisking well before adding the next one.

Add the wet ingredients to the dry ingredients and mix until just combined. Scoop out golf ball–size dough rounds and use your hands to roll the dough into a ball, then flatten to ¼ inch (6 mm) thick. Add a Rolo candy to the center and wrap the dough up around the candy. Roll this into an even ball, then roll it into the confectioners' sugar until heavily coated. Repeat with the remaining dough and candy.

Place the cookies 2 inches/5 cm apart on the prepared baking sheets and bake for 8 to 10 minutes, until the cookies look crinkly and have spread slightly. Let sit on the baking sheets for 5 minutes before transferring to a wire rack to cool briefly. Make sure to serve warm to get the gooey caramel.

ROCKY ROAD COOKIES

It's hard to imagine a more popular bake sale sweet than a crispy rice cereal treat or chocolate chip cookie, and yet, you're looking at it. Maybe it's the toasted marshmallow top or the big chunks of chocolate and walnuts tucked into a soft, chewy cookie, but no need to wonder: just make a batch and watch them disappear.

MAKES 18 TO 20 COOKIES

4 tablespoons (55 g) unsalted butter

7 ounces (200 g) bittersweet chocolate, chopped

¼ cup (20 g) unsweetened cocoa powder, sifted

3 large eggs, at room temperature

1 cup (200 g) granulated sugar

1 teaspoon pure vanilla extract

¼ teaspoon salt

¼ cup (30 g) all-purpose flour

¾ cup (95 g) roasted salted almonds, chopped

1 cup (45 g) mini marshmallows

21

Directions

Preheat the oven to 350°F (180°C). Line two baking sheets with parchment paper.

In a medium saucepan over medium heat, melt the butter. Remove from the heat and add the bittersweet chocolate and cocoa powder. Let sit for 30 seconds, then whisk the mixture until smooth. Set aside.

In a large bowl, using an electric mixer on medium speed, mix together the eggs, sugar, vanilla, and salt until light and fluffy and the mixture becomes pale in color, 3 to 4 minutes. Add the chocolate mixture and mix until just combined. Sift in the flour and fold in until just combined. Fold in the almonds quickly and carefully scoop golf ball–size mounds of dough onto the prepared baking sheets, at least 2 inches/5 cm apart.

Gently press 5 marshmallows into each cookie, then bake for 8 to 10 minutes, until the marshmallows are toasty and the cookies have spread. The cookies will appear slightly underbaked. Let cool on the baking sheets for 5 minutes before transferring to a wire rack to cool completely.

APPLE PECAN GRANOLA

I will clear off a shelf of boxed cereal for homemade granola anytime. It's the ideal snacking bite: sweet, savory, crunchy, and so easy to eat by the handful. If you think about it—despite its "healthy" disguise—granola is really just a deconstructed cookie, making it a great canvas for any kinds of add-ins that you'd normally save for a baked treat. To keep this recipe from being too loose, I added some brown rice syrup to help it clump—this way you can eat it as "almost" mini cookie bites. Try tossing it on top of just about anything from yogurt to ice cream, and even blitzing it into a smoothie. Feel free to swap in your favorite nuts or dried fruit!

MAKES 6 CUPS GRANOLA

1   cup (130 g) pecan halves, chopped

3   cups (300 g) old-fashioned rolled oats

½   cup (70 g) sunflower seeds

1½ teaspoons kosher salt

1½ teaspoons ground cinnamon

¼   teaspoon ground allspice

¼   teaspoon ground cardamom

½   cup (125 ml) olive oil

¼   cup (65 ml) honey

¼   cup (65 ml) brown rice syrup

2   teaspoons pure vanilla extract

½   cup (45 g) sweetened shredded coconut

1   cup (110 g) sliced almonds

1½ ounces (42 g) dried apples, diced

Directions

Preheat the oven to 325°F (165°C). Line a baking sheet with parchment paper.

Spread the pecans on the baking sheet and bake until toasted and golden, 5 to 7 minutes. Remove from the oven and transfer to a bowl. Set aside to cool, reserving the prepared baking sheet.

In a large bowl, whisk together the oats, sunflower seeds, salt, cinnamon, allspice, and cardamom. Stir in the olive oil, honey, brown rice syrup, and vanilla.

Transfer the oat mixture to the prepared baking sheet and press into a single layer. Bake undisturbed for about 30 minutes, or until the mixture is lightly browned and toasted in appearance. (For a looser granola, stir the mixture every 15 minutes.)

Sprinkle the coconut on top and bake for another 10 minutes. Remove the granola from the oven and stir in the almonds, dried apples, and toasted pecans. Set aside to cool completely on the baking sheet before serving or storing.

Store the granola in an airtight container for up to 7 days, at room temperature. Store in the refrigerator to extend the granola to 14 days.

SALTED DARK CHOCOLATE CHIP and ROASTED PECAN COOKIES

When it comes to chocolate chip cookies, everyone has a go-to favorite—crispy, doughy, bite-size, head size, and so forth. Well, this is mine: giant bakery style chocolate chip cookies dressed with dark chocolate, a double hit of pecan—pecan flour and chopped pecans—toasted coconut, and a touch of molasses to keep the cookies chewy. Sure, it's a little more work to toast and process a portion of the pecans to make pecan flour, but the combination of that and the toasted coconut is the secret to setting this chocolate chip cookie recipe apart from all the others. So, while I'm usually all about ingredient mixing and matching, I have to insist on this one that you stick with the recipe. I promise you won't be disappointed!

MAKES 16 GIANT BAKERY-STYLE (4-INCH/10 CM) COOKIES

1½ cups plus 2 tablespoons (145 g) sweetened shredded coconut

2¼ cups (290 g) pecan halves, divided

2 cups (240 g) all-purpose flour

¾ teaspoon baking soda

½ teaspoon salt

1 cup (225 g) unsalted butter, at room temperature

¾ cup plus 2 tablespoons (160 g) lightly packed brown sugar

½ cup (100 g) granulated sugar

1 large egg, at room temperature

1 large egg yolk, at room temperature

2 teaspoons pure vanilla extract

1½ teaspoons molasses

12 ounces (340 g) semisweet chocolate, chopped into ½-inch (1.3 cm) chunks

Directions

Preheat the oven to 350°F (180°C). Line two baking sheets with parchment paper. Spread the coconut on 1 sheet and the pecans on the other. Bake until lightly toasted, 5 to 7 minutes. Remove from the oven and transfer the baking sheets to a wire rack to cool completely.

Once cooled, roughly chop the coconut and set aside. For the pecans, to make the pecan flour, portion out ¾ cup/68 g and pulse in a food processor to a fine crumb; set aside. Roughly chop the remaining 1½ cups/150 g and set aside.

In a bowl, sift together the flour, baking soda, and salt. Whisk in the coconut and pecan flour. Set aside.

In a large bowl, using an electric mixer on medium speed, beat together the butter and both sugars until the mixture is light and fluffy, 3 to 5 minutes. Beat in the egg, mixing until fully combined. Add the yolk and beat until fully combined, followed by the vanilla

and molasses. Add the flour mixture all at once and beat on low speed, until the dough just comes together and flour streaks are still visible. Using a wooden spoon, finish mixing the dough manually. Fold in the chopped chocolate and reserved chopped pecans. Transfer the dough to the refrigerator to chill for at least 3 hours.

When ready to bake, preheat the oven to 350°F (180°C). Line two baking sheets with parchment paper.

Scoop out about 3 tablespoons/85 g of dough and flatten the dough onto the parchment-lined baking sheets to form a 3-inch/7.5 cm disk, ½ inch/1.3 cm thick. Continue to form cookies on each baking sheet, spacing the disks 1 inch/2.5 cm apart.

Bake the cookies until lightly browned, 10 to 12 minutes. Allow to cool for 3 minutes on the baking sheets, then transfer to a wire rack to cool completely.

CHOCOLATE MOUSSE FUDGE BROWNIES

My husband doesn't have much of a sweet tooth, but when it hollers, he goes for classic desserts like this. Sometimes with the mousse topping, sometimes without, but he never misses the opportunity to flavor his milk with brownie crumbs from repeated dunking.

MAKES 6 TO 8 SERVINGS

For the brownies

1   cup (90 g) unsweetened cocoa powder

1   cup (120 g) all-purpose flour

1   teaspoon baking powder

¼   teaspoon salt

1   cup (225 g) unsalted butter, melted

1½ cups (300 g) granulated sugar

3   large eggs, at room temperature

1   teaspoon pure vanilla extract

1   teaspoon instant espresso powder

½   cup (65 g) pecans or hazelnuts, chopped (optional)

For the chocolate mousse

1   cup (240 ml) heavy whipping cream

½   cup (60 g) confectioners' sugar

¼   cup (20 g) unsweetened cocoa powder

¼   teaspoon salt

Directions

Preheat the oven to 350°F (180°C). Line an 8-inch/20.5 cm square baking pan with parchment paper.

TO MAKE THE BROWNIES: In a medium bowl, whisk together the cocoa powder, flour, baking powder, and salt.

In a second medium bowl, mix together the butter, sugar, eggs, vanilla, and espresso powder. Add the flour mixture and mix well, being careful not to overmix. Fold in the pecans or hazelnuts, if using. Pour the batter into the prepared baking pan and bake for 25 to 30 minutes, or until a toothpick inserted into the center barely comes out clean. Remove from the oven and allow to cool completely in the pan.

TO MAKE THE CHOCOLATE MOUSSE: In a large bowl, combine the cream, confectioners' sugar, cocoa powder, and salt. Using an electric mixer on medium speed, beat until light and fluffy, 1 to 2 minutes.

Top the brownie layer with the chocolate mousse frosting.

DARK CHOCOLATE and CRANBERRY OATMEAL COOKIES

Don't be fooled by the humble appearance of these oat-meal cookies. The dark chocolate and cranberry pairing turns the standard comfort cookie into a real addiction.

MAKES 3 DOZEN COOKIES

1⅓ cups (175 g) all-purpose flour

½ teaspoon baking soda

⅛ teaspoon salt

¼ teaspoon ground cardamom

1 cup (225 g) unsalted butter, cubed, divided

1 cup (200 g) light brown sugar

⅔ cups (140 g) granulated sugar

2 teaspoons pure vanilla extract

2 large eggs, at room temperature

4 cups (400 g) old-fashioned rolled oats

1 cup (170 g) semisweet or bittersweet chocolate chips

1 cup (120 g) dried cranberries

Directions

Preheat the oven to 350°F (180°C). Line two baking sheets with parchment paper.

In a small bowl, whisk together the flour, baking soda, salt, and cardamom. Set aside.

In a medium saucepan over low heat, melt half of the butter (½ cup/113 g). Remove the pan from the heat and add the remaining butter (½ cup/113 g) to let the residual heat melt it. Add the brown sugar, granulated sugar, and vanilla, and whisk to combine. Add the eggs, 1 at a time, making sure the first one is fully combined before adding the next one.

Add the wet ingredients to the dry ingredients and stir just until combined. Fold in the oats, chocolate chips, and cranberries.

Using a medium cookie scoop or a tablespoon, drop rounded tablespoons of dough onto the baking sheets, 2 inches/5 cm apart.

Bake for 10 to 12 minutes, or until the cookies are golden brown. The cookies will be slightly underbaked at this point, but they will continue to bake as they cool on the baking sheet. Let the cookies cool for 5 minutes on the baking sheet before transferring to a wire rack to cool completely.

SPECULOOS BROWNIE CAKE

This is the potluck/picnic/bake sale brownie everyone goes for. Maybe it's the fact that brownies are pretty much everyone's favorite baked treat, or maybe it's because this cakelike version is frosted with a speculoos cookie spread, a delicious store-bought concoction made from crumbled biscuits.

MAKES 6 TO 8 SERVINGS

For the brownie cake

Nonstick cooking spray

½ cup (113 g) unsalted butter

3½ ounces (100 g) bittersweet chocolate, chopped

1⅓ cups (270 g) lightly packed light brown sugar

1 teaspoon pure vanilla extract

½ teaspoon instant espresso powder

3 large eggs, at room temperature

½ cup (60 g) all-purpose flour

1 teaspoon baking powder

½ teaspoon salt

For the speculoos frosting

¾ cup (205 g) speculoos cookie butter

6 tablespoons (85 g) unsalted butter, at room temperature

⅔ cup (70 g) confectioners' sugar

¼ teaspoon salt

2 tablespoons heavy whipping cream

Chocolate shavings, for garnish

Directions

TO MAKE THE BROWNIE CAKE: Preheat the oven to 350°F (180°C). Lightly coat a 9-inch/23 cm springform pan with nonstick cooking spray.

In a medium saucepan over medium heat, melt the butter. Remove the pan from the heat, add the bitter-sweet chocolate, and let sit for about 30 seconds, then whisk it all together until smooth and glossy. Add the brown sugar, vanilla, and espresso powder and whisk until smooth. Whisk in the eggs, 1 at a time, then sprinkle in the flour, baking powder, and salt. Use a sturdy spatula to fold it all together until there is no flour visible.

Spread the brownie mixture in the prepared spring-form pan and bake for 20 to 25 minutes, or until the cake has puffed slightly and the top is shiny and just barely cracked. Transfer to a wire rack to cool completely before removing the sides of the springform pan. In the meantime, make the speculoos frosting.

TO MAKE THE SPECULOOS FROSTING: In a large bowl, using an electric mixer on medium speed, mix together the speculoos and butter for a full minute so it's light and fluffy. Add the confectioners' sugar, salt, and cream and beat for another minute, or until the mixture is fluffy and spreadable.

Spread the frosting on the cake, garnish with chocolate shavings, and cut into wedges to serve.

NO-BAKE BANANA
and COCONUT COOKIES

A no-bake cookie, you say? Raise your eyebrows if you will, but just know that these cookies are not only incredibly easy to make but are also incredibly delicious. I often make them with almond butter, but any nut butter (in equal measure) will work.

MAKES ABOUT 2 DOZEN COOKIES

1   cup (200 g) granulated sugar

⅓   cup (75 ml) milk

4   tablespoons (55 g) unsalted butter

1   tablespoon molasses

1½ cups (150 g) old-fashioned rolled oats

½   cup (40 g) sweetened shredded coconut

½   cup (70 g) freeze-dried banana slices, finely chopped

½   cup (135 g) almond butter

1   tablespoon pure vanilla extract

   Pinch of kosher salt

Directions

Line a baking sheet with parchment or waxed paper.

In a medium saucepan over medium heat, bring the sugar, milk, butter, and molasses to a boil, then boil for 1 minute, stirring occasionally. Remove from the heat. Stir in the oats, coconut, banana slices, almond butter, vanilla, and salt.

Drop tablespoons of the mixture onto the prepared baking sheet. Let sit at room temperature until cooled and hardened, about 1 hour.

CAMPFIRE GRANOLA BARS

When I was in my twenties, granola was everything. I worked at a health food store that sold what seemed like a dozen-plus varieties in bulk bins. I ate it for breakfast, for lunch, for dinner, for a snack, for, well, all day long. It was budget-friendly (hello, employee discount!), but then I discovered I could make it on my own and make it my own. This is one of the first versions I made, and it's still my favorite. It has seen several iterations over the years, but this original bar form version—which is super-on-the-go-friendly—tends to be made the most. That said, you can definitely leave it loose to sprinkle on top of yogurt or ice cream, or just eat by the handfuls.

MAKES 12 TO 16 BARS

Nonstick cooking spray

3 cups (300 g) old-fashioned rolled oats

1 cup (90 g) sliced almonds

½ cup (113 g) unsalted butter

⅔ cup (210 g) honey

¼ cup (55 g) packed light brown sugar

¼ teaspoon salt

2 teaspoons pure vanilla extract

8 graham crackers (35 g), broken up into small pieces

1 cup (170 g) semisweet or bittersweet chocolate chips

1 cup (45 g) mini marshmallows

Directions

Preheat the oven to 350°F (180°C). Line a 13 x 9-inch/ 33 x 23 cm baking pan with parchment paper, leaving a 2-inch/5 cm overhang on 2 opposite sides, then spray with nonstick cooking spray.

In a large bowl, combine the oats and almonds. Spread the mixture on a separate, ungreased baking sheet and toast for 10 minutes, or until the oats and almonds become fragrant and light brown. Transfer the oat mixture back to the bowl.

In a medium saucepan over medium heat, bring the butter, honey, brown sugar, and salt to a boil. Remove from the heat and stir in the vanilla.

Pour the honey mixture over the oat mixture and stir to combine. Fold in the graham cracker pieces, chocolate chips, and mini marshmallows.

Spoon the mixture into the prepared pan and bake for 20 minutes, or until just golden brown. Remove from the oven, allow the granola bars to cool completely in the pan, then cut into rectangles. Use the paper overhang to help lift the bars out of the pan.

CARAMEL POPCORN COOKIES

It's hard to put my finger on what exactly I like best about these cookies—maybe it's their caramelly brown-butter flavor; or it's the soft and chewy center with a crisp, caramelized edge; or it could be the delightful don't-have-to-choose-just-one idea that I can mix caramel popcorn (and lots of chocolate and butterscotch chips) with a delicious cookie.

MAKES 30 COOKIES

- 3 cups (300 g) store-bought or homemade caramel corn, divided
- 1¾ cups (210 g) all-purpose flour
- 2 teaspoons baking soda
- ½ teaspoon salt
- ¾ cup (170 g) unsalted butter, at room temperature
- 1 cup (215 g) lightly packed light brown sugar
- ¼ cup (50 g) granulated sugar
- 1½ teaspoons pure vanilla extract
- 1 large egg, at room temperature
- ½ cup (90 g) butterscotch chips, roughly chopped

Directions

Preheat the oven to 350°F (180°C). Line a baking sheet with parchment paper and set aside.

Prepare the caramel corn by roughly chopping 1 cup/100 g; set aside. Then, finely chop the remaining 2 cups/200 g of caramel corn by hand on a cutting board (using the food processor could cause the caramel corn to stick together in clumps); set aside. In a bowl, whisk together the flour, baking soda, and salt.

In a large bowl, using an electric mixer on medium speed, cream together the butter, both sugars, and vanilla until pale and fluffy, 2 to 3 minutes. Add the egg and beat until combined. Add the flour and mix on low speed, just until no flour streaks are visible. Using a wooden spoon, fold in the roughly chopped caramel corn and the chopped butterscotch chips.

Using a small cookie scoop or a tablespoon, drop rounded tablespoons of dough into the finely chopped caramel corn to coat. Place each coated ball on the prepared baking sheet, leaving 2 inches/5 cm of space between them. (You will need to bake them in batches.)

Bake for 8 to 10 minutes, until lightly golden brown.

Remove from the oven, let the cookies cool on the baking sheet for 5 minutes, and then transfer to a wire rack to cool completely.

APRICOT COCONUT BARS

Apricot season is way too short, so the moment they appear at the market, this is the first recipe I reach for. I love how the naturally sweet and tart flavor of the apricots plays against the rich shortbread crust and the coconut topping. Although, I'm also just as happy making this with other stone fruits, or even berries. The ratios stay the same, but the baking times will vary.

These are best served after being chilled and set in the refrigerator for easy cutting.

MAKES ABOUT 16 BARS

For the shortbread crust

1   cup (120 g) all-purpose flour

¼   cup (53 g) packed light brown sugar

¼   teaspoon salt

½   cup (113 g) cold unsalted butter, cut into ½-inch (1.3 cm) cubes

1   tablespoon cold water

For the apricot filling

1½   pounds (680 g) fresh apricots, pitted and quartered

½   cup (100 g) granulated sugar

½   cup (110 g) packed light brown sugar

2   tablespoons cornstarch

2   teaspoons pure vanilla extract

Pinch of salt

For the coconut topping

1   cup (120 g) all-purpose flour

1   cup (85 g) sweetened shredded coconut

½   cup (113 g) unsalted butter, at room temperature, cut into cubes

½   cup (110 g) packed light brown sugar

¼   teaspoon salt

47

Directions

Preheat the oven to 350°F (180°C). Line an 8-inch/20.5 cm square baking pan with parchment paper, allowing 2 inches/5 cm of overhang on 2 opposite sides.

TO MAKE THE SHORTBREAD CRUST: In a food processor, pulse to combine the flour, sugar, and salt. Add the butter and pulse until combined. Then, add the water and pulse until the dough has come together and stays together when you squeeze it with your hand. Press the dough into the bottom of the prepared pan and bake for 15 to 20 minutes, or until the dough is a light golden brown. Remove from the oven and set aside to cool.

TO MAKE THE APRICOT FILLING: In a medium bowl, combine the apricots, both sugars, and the cornstarch, vanilla, and salt. Set aside.

TO MAKE THE COCONUT TOPPING: In the same food processor as was used for the crust, combine the flour, coconut, butter, brown sugar, and salt. Pulse until crumbly but not dry. If it is dry, continue to pulse until the butter is more incorporated and the crumble has come together.

Assemble the bars by pouring the apricot mixture on top of the baked crust in an even layer. Top with the coconut crumble. Bake for about 1 hour, or until the apricot mixture is bubbling, tenting with foil after 30 minutes to prevent the topping from burning. Remove from the oven and transfer to a wire rack to cool completely. Cut into bars and serve, using the paper overhang to help lift the bars out of the pan.

MONSTER COOKIE BARK

If you are a fan of those trendy, thin, barklike brownie squares, you are going to love this confectionary mash-up. It has a crispy base, but instead of chocolate, it's a cookie—complete with all the candy fixin's of a monster cookie.

MAKES 1 (13 X 10-INCH/33 X 25.5 CM) SLAB

⅓ cup plus 2 tablespoons (55 g) all-purpose flour

⅓ cup (30 g) old-fashioned rolled oats

¼ teaspoon salt

¼ teaspoon baking soda

2 large egg whites, at room temperature

1 teaspoon pure vanilla extract

4 tablespoons (55 g) unsalted butter, melted and slightly cooled

1 cup (200 g) granulated sugar

2 cups (350 g) semisweet chocolate chips, divided

¾ cup (55 g) mini M&M's

2 ounces (56 g) chopped pretzels

3 tablespoons confectioners' sugar (for dusting)

Directions

Preheat the oven to 325°F (165°C). Line a 15 x 10-inch/38 x 25.5 cm jelly-roll pan with parchment.

In a medium bowl, combine the flour, oats, salt, and baking soda. Set aside.

In a large bowl, using an electric mixer on medium speed and increasing to medium-high speed after 30 seconds, beat the egg whites until frothy, about 2 minutes (if they start to shrink in the bowl, stop immediately). Stir together vanilla extract and butter. Slowly add the butter mixture to the egg mixture by pouring it down the side of the mixer bowl. Beat on low speed until just combined, scraping the bottom of the bowl as needed to make sure there is no unincorporated butter. Add the sugar and beat for another 30 seconds to blend. Fold in the flour mixture until just combined. Fold in 1 cup/175 g of the chocolate chips, and the M&M's and pretzels.

Spread the mixture on the prepared jelly-roll pan. Bake for 20 to 25 minutes, or until the bark is cooked through and does not give when gently pressed in the center. Remove from the oven and place on a wire rack to cool completely. Once cooled, place a matching pan on top of the cookie crust and flip over so the bottom side is now facing up. Set aside.

In a microwave-safe bowl, melt the remaining cup/175 g of chocolate chips in a microwave on MEDIUM-HIGH in 5-second bursts, making sure to stir between each burst (or melt in a double boiler). Using an offset spatula, spread the melted chocolate across the bark. Allow the chocolate to set, dust with confectioners' sugar, and then cut the bark into large chunks, using a knife.

CHOCOLATE and RASPBERRY OOEY-GOOEY BARS

This is a spin-off of the classic ooey-gooey bar. If you are familiar with the southern classic, then you know of its signature—slightly overpowering—corn syrupy sweetness—something that always keeps you from having more than one piece. But this version has more subtle sweetness with a chocolate crust and the addition of fresh raspberries.

MAKES 8 TO 10 BARS

1 cup (225 g) unsalted butter, melted and slightly cooled, plus more for pan

3 large eggs, at room temperature, divided

1 (15.25-ounce/432 g) box chocolate cake mix

8 ounces (226 g) cream cheese, at room temperature

1½ teaspoons pure vanilla extract

1 pound (453 g) confectioners' sugar, plus 2 tablespoons for dusting

⅓ cup (55 g) bittersweet chocolate chips

1⅓ cups (170 g) fresh raspberries

Preheat the oven to 350°F (180°C). Lightly grease a 13 x 9-inch/33 x 23 cm baking pan with butter and set aside.

In a large bowl, combine the butter and 1 egg. Stir in the dry chocolate cake mix and press the resulting dough into the bottom of the prepared pan to form a crust. Set aside.

In a large bowl, using an electric mixer on medium-high speed, beat the cream cheese until smooth, about 30 seconds. Add the remaining 2 eggs and the vanilla and continue to beat until combined, scraping down the sides of the bowl as needed. Add the confectioners' sugar and beat on low speed until fully combined, 2 to 3 minutes. Pour the batter over the crust.

In a microwave-safe bowl, melt the chocolate in a microwave on MEDIUM-HIGH in 5-second bursts, stirring between bursts, until the chocolate is fully melted (or melt in a double boiler). Drizzle the chocolate on top of the cream cheese batter. Drag a knife through the chocolate and batter in a zigzag pattern to marble it.

Sprinkle the raspberries on top and bake for 25 to 30 minutes, or until a toothpick inserted into the center barely comes out clean. Remove from the oven and transfer to a wire rack to cool. Dust with confectioners' sugar and cut into bars.

CHOCOLATE-DIPPED ORANGE and EARL GREY SHORTBREAD COOKIES

Shortbread always reminds me of those Danish butter cookies that come in a blue tin, which were the closest thing to Christmas cookies in my home when I was a kid. As a result, making plain shortbread cookies is my annual homage to my childhood, but not without also making some fun and interesting variations like this one. The orange zest gives the cookie just a bit of zip, while the infused Earl Grey tea lends a subtle, floral-like flavor (and no shortage of elegance). To dip or not to dip in chocolate—that's up to you. It's a great cookie, either way.

MAKES 12 CHOCOLATE-DIPPED SHORTBREAD BARS

¾ cup (170 g) unsalted butter, at room temperature

1 cup (120 g) confectioners' sugar

2 teaspoons loose Earl Grey tea leaves

1½ teaspoons orange zest

¾ teaspoon salt

2 cups (240 g) all-purpose flour

7 ounces (200 g) bittersweet or semisweet chocolate, chopped

Sanding sugar, sprinkles, or flaky sea salt (all optional)

Directions

Preheat the oven to 350°F (180°C) and line an 8-inch/ 20.5 cm square baking pan, leaving a 1-inch/2.5 cm over- hang on opposite sides.

In a large bowl, using an electric mixer on high speed, cream the butter, confectioners' sugar, tea leaves, orange zest, and salt until the mixture is light and fluffy and slightly paler in color than when you started, 3 to 5 min- utes. Add the flour and mix on low speed just until the dough comes together. Press it evenly into the prepared pan and bake until the edges are lightly golden brown, 25 to 30 minutes. Remove from the oven and transfer to a wire rack to cool completely in the pan.

Use the paper overhang to help lift the cooled short bread from the pan, cut into 6 long bars, and then cut those in half to get 12 bars.

Place the chocolate in a heatproof bowl over barely simmering water, making sure the bottom of the bowl isn't touching the water, and melt, stirring occasionally.

Dip half of each shortbread bar into the melted choc- olate, then transfer to a parchment-lined baking sheet. Sprinkle with any of the toppings, if using, or leave plain. Transfer the bars to the refrigerator for the chocolate to set, then serve.

KITCHEN SINK COOKIE BARS

This is the recipe to grab when your pantry is full of bits and pieces, odds and ends, and just about anything else you want to throw in this cookie bar.

MAKES ABOUT 24 BARS

Nonstick cooking spray

2 cups (240 g) all-purpose flour

1 teaspoon baking soda

1 teaspoon salt

1 cup (225 g) unsalted butter, at room temperature

1½ cups (315 g) lightly packed brown sugar

2 large eggs, at room temperature

1 tablespoon pure vanilla extract

2 cups (260 g) pecan halves, toasted and chopped

8 ounces (226 g) semisweet or bittersweet chocolate, roughly chopped

2 cups (200 g) old-fashioned rolled oats

2 cups (170 g) unsweetened shredded coconut

Directions

Preheat the oven to 350°F (180°C). Spray a 13 x 9-inch/ 33 x 23 cm baking pan with nonstick cooking spray.

In a small bowl, whisk together the flour, baking soda, and salt. Set aside.

In a large bowl, using an electric mixer on medium-high speed, combine the butter and brown sugar and beat until light and fluffy, 3 to 5 minutes. On low speed, beat in the eggs, 1 at a time, then the vanilla. Scrape the sides and bottom of the bowl. Slowly add the flour mixture, beating on low speed until just barely combined. Fold in the pecans, chopped chocolate, oats, and coconut.

Spread the batter in the prepared pan and bake for 30 to 35 minutes, or until golden brown. Remove from the oven and allow to cool completely in the pan, then cut into bars.

PIES AND TARTS

I was pretty late getting on the band-wagon when it came to making pies and tarts. That's most likely because as a kid, the only kind I knew had soggy crusts and gelatinous fillings and were typically way too sweet. But, determined to be a well-rounded baker, I tackled them. After a few rounds of tough crusts and watery fillings, I got it. I got it so much that I never stopped. Now every time summer comes around, all that fresh fruit bounty is destined for family gather-ings in pie or tart form.

BLACKBERRY CRUMBLE PIE

When I first started baking, I never understood the term "easy as pie." Sure, making the filling was simple enough, but the crust was always a challenge. I had a tendency to overwork what should have been a tender, flaky crust into something that more closely resembled Play-Doh in texture. So, I started by making buckles and crumbles instead—they have all the deliciousness of fruit pie, without the hassle of rolling out dough.

MAKES 6 TO 8 SERVINGS

Nonstick cooking spray

For the topping

3½ ounces (100 g) almond paste

⅓ cup (70 g) granulated sugar

1 cup (120 g) all-purpose flour

¼ teaspoon salt

½ cup (113 g) cold unsalted butter, cut into ½-inch (1.3 cm) cubes

⅓ cup (30 g) old-fashioned oats

For the filling

2 pounds (1 kg) fresh or frozen blackberries

⅓ cup (70 g) granulated sugar

3 tablespoons all-purpose flour

2 tablespoons freshly squeezed lemon juice

Directions

Preheat the oven to 350°F (180°C) and lightly grease a 13 x 9-inch/33 x 23 cm baking pan with nonstick cooking spray.

TO MAKE THE TOPPING: Combine the almond paste and sugar in a food processor and pulse until the texture of sand is achieved. Add the flour and salt and pulse once or twice to combine. Add the cold butter and pulse until the butter is incorporated and the size of small peas. (Alternatively, use a pastry blender to combine.)

Add the oats and pulse or stir once to combine, then transfer the mixture to the fridge to chill while you make the filling.

TO MAKE THE BLACKBERRY FILLING: In a large bowl, combine the blackberries, sugar, flour, and lemon juice; stir until well blended. Transfer the mixture to the prepared baking pan. Using your hands, break up the crumble and sprinkle it evenly over the top of the filling.

Bake until the top is lightly golden brown and the filling is bubbling, 35 to 40 minutes. Serve warm with vanilla ice cream.

PEACH and BOURBON LATTICE PIE

Peach pie is a summer tradition in my family, but before the pie came out of the oven, there were just the glorious peaches—stealing them from our neighbor's low-lying branches, and running through the yard with sticky fingers and stained T-shirts. These days I'm not doing too much peach poaching, but I am, without fail, making this pie. The pairing of bourbon and peach is a little bit of a departure from the classic summer staple, but I love the way the bourbon brings out the deep sweetness of the peaches. Don't worry if peaches aren't in season—frozen is a totally acceptable option, as those peaches are picked and flash-frozen at their peak ripeness. Simply defrost them before using.

MAKES 6 TO 8 SERVINGS

2½ pounds (1.1 kg) fresh peaches (5 to 6 peaches), pitted and sliced in ½-inch (1.3 cm) slices

½ cup (105 g) lightly packed light brown sugar

¼ cup (30 g) cornstarch

1½ tablespoons bourbon

1¼ teaspoons vanilla bean paste

¼ teaspoon salt

2 recipes Pie Dough (page 100), divided

1 large egg whisked with 1 teaspoon water

Turbinado sugar, for sprinkling

Directions

Make the filling by placing the peaches, brown sugar, cornstarch, bourbon, vanilla bean paste, and salt in a large bowl, mixing just until everything is combined. Set aside.

Roll out one of the pie dough disks to ¼ inch/6 mm thick, placing it in a 9-inch/23 cm pie pan, leaving a 1-inch/2.5 cm overhang around the edge. Transfer it to the refrigerator to chill while the top crust is rolled out.

Create a lattice top crust from the remaining portion of pie dough: roll out the dough to ⅛-inch/3 mm thickness, and cut into 1-inch/2.5 cm-wide strips. Drain and add the filling to the pastry lined pie pan. Starting from the left, lay one strip across the pie, then lay a second strip perpendicular to it. Weave the third strip underneath the perpendicular strip, and keep going in this pattern, weaving over and under strips of lattice. Trim the edges flush with the rim, and press the top and bottom edges together, crimping decoratively. Brush the entire pie with egg wash and sprinkle with turbinado sugar.

Place the pie in the freezer to chill while the oven preheats to 375°F (190°C). Remove from the freezer and set the pie pan on a baking sheet. Bake until the crust is browned and the filling is bubbling, 50 to 55 minutes. Check the pie after 30 minutes and cover the top and edges with foil if they are becoming too dark. Remove from the oven and place on a wire rack to cool for at least 3 hours before serving.

LEMON RICOTTA CHEESECAKE *with* FRESH BERRIES

Whenever I need to bring something to a party, this is my go-to cake. Not only does it not need babysitting on your lap when you're en route, but it also has the loveliest yellow color. Oh yeah, and it tastes amazing—rich and decadent, yet bright. You can make it up to three days in advance and macerate the berries on the day you're serving the cake.

MAKES 8 TO 10 SERVINGS

Nonstick cooking spray

6 ounces (170 g) graham crackers (about 12 crackers)

1½ cups (300 g) granulated sugar, divided

Salt

6 tablespoons (86 g) unsalted butter, melted

4 cups (960 ml) whole-milk ricotta cheese

¼ cup (30 g) all-purpose flour

4 large eggs, at room temperature

2 teaspoons pure vanilla extract

¼ cup (60 ml) freshly squeezed lemon juice, divided

2 tablespoons freshly grated lemon zest

2 pints (340 g) fresh berries, such as strawberries, blueberries, or blackberries

1 sprig fresh mint

Directions

Preheat the oven to 350°F (180°C). Spray a 9-inch/23 cm springform pan with nonstick cooking spray.

In a food processor, pulse the graham crackers and 2 tablespoons of the sugar until the graham crackers are finely ground. Add ¼ teaspoon of salt and the melted butter and pulse until the graham cracker mixture has the texture of wet sand, 5 to 7 pulses. Press the graham cracker mixture evenly into the bottom of the prepared springform pan.

Bake for about 10 minutes, or until the crust is golden brown. Remove from the oven and set aside to cool completely. Lower the oven temperature to 325°F (165°C).

In a clean food processor, process the ricotta until very smooth and creamy. Add 1 cup/200 g of the sugar, the flour, and a pinch of salt and pulse until combined. Add the eggs, vanilla, lemon zest, and 2 tablespoons of the lemon juice and pulse until completely incorporated. Pour the filling into the cooled graham cracker crust and bake for 60 to 75 minutes, or until the filling puffs up and the center only slightly jiggles when the pan is gently shaken. Remove from the oven and place on a wire rack to cool completely.

In a bowl, combine the berries, the remaining 9 tablespoons/90 g of sugar, and the remaining 2 tablespoons of lemon juice. Allow the berries to macerate for about 30 minutes.

When ready to serve, remove the sides of the pan and top the cheesecake with the macerated berries and mint.

GRAHAM DUTCH APPLE PIE

There's something about apple pie that makes us nostalgic: everyone has a fond memory associated with it. Mine is of making my very first one, because it was also the first pie I had ever attempted. I was so worried about getting the crust right that the filling was pretty much an afterthought. So much so that the perfectly mandoline-sliced apples still had the produce stickers on them! These days, I only have to worry about making sure that I have enough—this pie is a family favorite that never lasts long. Everyone loves the piled-high apple slices topped with the crunchy graham cracker streusel.

MAKES 8 TO 10 SERVINGS

1   recipe Pie Dough (page 100)

For the streusel

1   cup (100 g) graham cracker crumbs (from about 6 crackers)

½   cup (60 g) all-purpose flour

⅓   cup (70 g) lightly packed light brown sugar

¼   teaspoon salt

½   cup (113 g) cold unsalted butter, cut into cubes

For the filling

3   pounds (1.4 kg) Pink Lady apples, peeled, cored, and cut into 1-inch/2.5 cm pieces (6 to 8 apples)

½   cup (105 g) light brown sugar

¼   cup (30 g) cornstarch

1½   teaspoons ground cinnamon

¼   teaspoon ground allspice

¼   teaspoon salt

1   large egg mixed with 1 teaspoon water

Directions

Preheat the oven to 375°F (190°C). Roll out the pie dough to ¼ inch/6 mm thick, placing it in a 9-inch/23 cm pie pan and crimping it however you prefer. Place in the freezer to chill while you prepare the rest of the pie.

TO MAKE THE STREUSEL: Pulse together the graham cracker crumbs, flour, brown sugar, and salt. Add the butter and pulse just until it starts to look like small peas. Transfer to the refrigerator to chill while you prepare the filling.

TO MAKE THE FILLING: Toss the apple slices with the brown sugar, cornstarch, cinnamon, allspice, and salt.

Place the filling in the prepared crust, then cover with the streusel. Brush the egg wash onto the edges of the piecrust and bake for 35 to 40 minutes, until the crust and streusel topping are golden brown. Remove from the oven and allow to cool on a wire rack for at least 1 hour before serving or refrigerate for at least 30 minutes for perfectly cut slices.

GRAPEFRUIT and VANILLA BEAN PANNA COTTA TART

I'm a big fan of panna cotta because it's a great way to highlight just about any ingredient. One of my favorite additions, though, is fruit—particularly citrus. The soft blush color of grapefruit—helped with a drop of pink food coloring, if you want—is just as dainty and fresh as this dessert tastes.

MAKES 6 TO 8 SERVINGS

1   recipe Tart Dough (page 101)
    All-purpose flour, for dusting

1¼ cups (300 ml) heavy whipping cream, divided

½   cup (100 g) granulated sugar, divided

¼   teaspoon salt

1   vanilla bean, split lengthwise, or 2 teaspoons pure vanilla extract

2½ teaspoons (about 1 packet) powdered gelatin

¾   cup (180 ml) pulp-free pink grapefruit juice (juice from about 2 large grapefruits, strained)

2   pink grapefruits, peeled and segmented

Directions

Preheat the oven to 375°F (190°C).

On a lightly floured surface, roll out the tart dough into a 12-inch/30.5 cm round about ¼ inch/6 mm thick. Roll the dough around the rolling pin and gently transfer to a 9-inch/23 cm tart pan. Carefully press the dough down onto the bottom and sides of the pan. Roll the rolling pin on top of the tart pan to score the circumference, then remove any excess dough. Cover the tart dough with foil and fill with pie weights. Bake the tart crust for 20 to 25 minutes. Remove the foil and pie weights and continue to bake for another 10 minutes, or until the crust is a golden brown. Remove from the oven and place on a wire rack to cool completely.

Combine 1 cup/240 ml of the cream and 6 tablespoons of the sugar and salt in a medium saucepan. Scrape the seeds out of the vanilla bean and add the seeds and the pod to the cream. Bring the cream to a simmer over medium heat, stirring constantly, then remove from the heat, cover with a lid, and allow the cream and vanilla to steep for 30 minutes.

In a small bowl, stir together the remaining ¼ cup/60 ml of cream and the gelatin. Set aside to allow the gelatin to bloom for 2 to 3 minutes.

Remove the vanilla bean from the cream mixture and bring the mixture to a low simmer over low heat. Remove from the heat, then add the gelatin mixture and grapefruit juice. Whisk until combined, then pour the grapefruit mixture into the cooled tart pan. Refrigerate until the panna cotta is firm, about 4 hours.

When ready to serve, stir together the grapefruit segments and remaining 2 tablespoons of sugar. Top the panna cotta with the grapefruit segments.

CHOCOLATE PEAR TART

Everyone needs a dessert like this in his or her repertoire. It's elegant in appearance yet rustic and homey
in flavor, and is the perfect way to finish off any dinner
party. While this recipe might look intimidating, it's
really quite easy to make. The key is slicing the pears as
evenly as possible so that it's easy to fan them out.

MAKES 6 TO 8 SERVINGS

   Nonstick cooking spray

⅔ cup (110 g) all-purpose flour

½ cup (50 g) unsweetened cocoa powder, sifted

¾ teaspoon ground ginger

½ teaspoon ground cinnamon

½ teaspoon salt

½ cup (113 g) unsalted butter, at room temperature

1 cup (200 g) granulated sugar

3 large eggs, at room temperature

½ cup (90 g) chopped semisweet chocolate

1½ to 2 (340 g) Anjou pears, cored, halved and sliced to
   ⅛-inch/3 mm thickness

   Confectioners' sugar, for dusting (optional)

Directions

Preheat the oven to 350°F (180°C). Lightly coat a 9-inch/ 23 cm round tart pan or a 5 x 14-inch/12.5 x 35.5 cm rectangular, removable-bottom tart pan with nonstick cooking spray.

In a medium bowl, whisk together the flour, cocoa powder, ginger, cinnamon, and salt. Set aside.

In a large bowl, using an electric mixer on medium speed, beat together the butter and granulated sugar until light and fluffy, 1 to 2 minutes, scraping down the side of the bowl. Then, add the eggs, 1 at a time, making sure each egg is mixed in before adding the next. Add the dry ingredients and mix on low speed until just combined. Fold in the chocolate and spread the batter evenly in the prepared pan.

Fan out the pears on top of the batter, being careful not to overlap too much, then bake for 20 to 25 minutes, until the tart is slightly puffed and a toothpick inserted away from the pears comes out clean. The area around the pear will be gooey and fudgy. Remove from the oven and place on a wire rack to cool for an hour before serving. Dust with confectioners' sugar, if desired.

STRAWBERRY and EARL GREY CREAM TART

This simple tart relies on having the freshest, sweetest strawberries, so take the extra care of sourcing the freshest (read: in-season) fruit you can. It's the perfect use for those soft, deep red berries that are almost unable to cope with their own sweetness. Equally important is the texture of the tart shell. Don't assemble the tarts until you're ready to serve them, or your crispy, flaky puff pastry will quickly turn flat and soggy. As a time-saver, you can make the whipped cream two days ahead and keep it chilled in the fridge. Then, use the time while the puff pastry is baking to prep the strawberries. Dessert in no time!

MAKES 6 SERVINGS

1   cup (225 ml) heavy whipping cream

1   tablespoon loose Earl Grey tea leaves

3   tablespoons honey

1   teaspoon vanilla bean paste

1   sheet store-bought puff pastry, thawed in the refrigerator overnight

All-purpose flour, for dusting

1   large egg, lightly beaten

Coarse sugar, for sprinkling

4   tablespoons high-quality strawberry jam

1   pound (454 g) strawberries

Directions

In a medium bowl, combine the cream and tea leaves. Cover with plastic wrap and chill for at least 2 hours to steep. Remove from the refrigerator and strain. Add the honey and vanilla paste to the tea-infused cream and beat with an electric mixer until soft peaks form. Cover and set aside.

Roll out the puff pastry to a 9-inch/23 cm square on a lightly floured surface. Cut the dough into three 9 x 3-inch/23 x 7.5 cm rectangles. Transfer the puff pastry to a parchment-lined baking sheet. Brush a ½-inch/1.3 cm border around the pastry with the beaten egg. Prick the pastry with a fork. Cover and chill in the refrigerator for 30 minutes.

While the pastry chills, preheat the oven to 400°F (200°C).

Remove the puff pastry from the refrigerator and lightly sprinkle with coarse sugar. Bake for 15 to 20 minutes, or until crisp and golden. Remove from the oven and place on a wire rack to cool completely.

To assemble: Place the jam with 1 tablespoon of water in a microwave-safe bowl. Microwave on MEDIUM in 10-second bursts, stirring between bursts, for a total of 30 seconds, or until the jam is well combined and is slightly thinned; set aside to cool. Hull the strawberries and slice into ¼-inch/6 mm slices. Transfer the tart crusts to a serving platter and spread the tea-infused cream on top, cover with sliced strawberries, and brush the strawberry layer with jam.

FLUFFERNUTTER TART

Fluffernutter sandwiches are a favorite after-school snack in my home. If I allowed it, they would probably eat them every day. Never one for repetition, but a sucker for my kids, I switch up the sandwich with handful of other peanut butter and marshmallow creme recipes, but this tart, with its toasted topping, always goes fastest.

MAKES 8 TO 10 SERVINGS

For the crust

- ½ cup (113 g) unsalted butter, melted
- 2 cups (200 g) graham cracker crumbs
- ¼ cup (55 g) lightly packed light brown sugar
- ¼ teaspoon salt

For the filling

- 1 cup (270 ml) creamy all-natural peanut butter
- 1⅔ cups (415 ml) heavy whipping cream
- ⅓ cup (40 g) confectioners' sugar, sifted
- 1 teaspoon pure vanilla extract

For the marshmallow creme

- 2 large egg whites
- 1 cup (200 g) granulated sugar
- ½ teaspoon pure vanilla extract
- ¼ teaspoon salt

Directions

Preheat the oven to 350°F (180°C).

TO MAKE THE CRUST: In a bowl, mix together the butter, graham cracker crumbs, brown sugar, and salt. Press the mixture into a 9-inch/23 cm removable-bottom tart pan. Bake the crust for 10 to 12 minutes, or until it starts to brown. Remove from the oven and let cool completely.

TO MAKE THE FILLING: In a bowl, beat together the peanut butter, cream, confectioners' sugar, and vanilla until well combined, 1 to 2 minutes. Scrape the filling into the baked crust and evenly smooth out the top. Transfer to the refrigerator to chill while you make the fluff.

TO MAKE THE MARSHMALLOW CREME: In a large bowl, combine the egg whites, granulated sugar, vanilla, and salt. Set the bowl over simmering water, making sure the water is not touching the bottom of the bowl. Clip a candy thermometer onto the side of the bowl. Cook the mixture, stirring, until the temperature reaches 160°F (71°C), 3 to 5 minutes. Remove the bowl from the heat and beat the mixture until it is fluffy, 5 to 7 minutes.

Using an offset spatula, spread the fluff over the peanut butter filling. Use a kitchen torch to lightly toast and brown the top.

BURNT CARAMEL CUSTARD PIE

Unlike most pie lovers, if I'm given a choice between a fruit- or custard-filled one, I always reach for the custard one first. The rich, custardy smoothness draws me in every time. This pie is no exception; the added brûléed sugar top gives the ensemble a slight crunch and added dimension in flavor.

MAKES 6 TO 8 SERVINGS

1   recipe Pie Dough (page 100)

4½ cups (1.1 L) heavy whipping cream, divided

1   vanilla bean, split lengthwise

¾   cup plus 2 tablespoons (175 g) granulated sugar, divided

4   large egg yolks, at room temperature

¼   teaspoon salt

     Flaky sea salt, for sprinkling

Directions

Preheat the oven to 350°F (180°C).

Roll out the pie dough and fit it into a 9-inch/23 cm pie pan. Trim the edges and create a decorative flute or crimped edge. Freeze for 30 minutes.

Line the crust with foil and pie weights. Bake until lightly browned and dry to the touch, about 20 minutes. Remove from the oven. Remove the foil and weights from the piecrust and place on a wire rack to cool completely. Lower the oven temperature to 325°F (165°C).

Bring 3 cups/710 ml of the cream and the vanilla bean and its seeds to a simmer in a medium saucepan over medium heat. Remove from the heat, cover with plastic wrap, and let the cream and vanilla bean steep for 20 to 30 minutes. Discard the vanilla bean.

Combine ¾ cup/150 g of the sugar and 2 tablespoons of water in a medium saucepan. Over medium-high heat, bring the mixture to a boil, stirring only until the sugar dissolves. Then, stop stirring and allow to boil until mixture turns a deep amber color, 3 to 4 minutes. Remove from the heat. Carefully and slowly whisk in the cream mixture to create caramel.

In a large bowl, whisk the egg yolks and salt. Whisking constantly, slowly stream in the caramel sauce. Pour the caramel mixture into the cooled piecrust and bake for 45 to 50 minutes, or until the caramel filling is only slightly jiggly in the center and the top is golden brown.

Remove from the oven and place on a wire rack to cool. Chill the pie until completely cool. When ready to serve, make the whipped cream by beating the remaining 1½ cups/354 ml of cream and remaining 2 tablespoons of sugar on high speed in a bowl until soft peaks form. Pile the whipped cream on top of the pie and sprinkle with sea salt.

SOUR CHERRY LIME PIE

Sour cherries have a short season and limited availability here in Southern California. So, naturally, it's also my favorite fruit—always craving the elusive: such a terrible character flaw! When I finally get my hands on some, I go crazy, stuffing them into every possible recipe. Sour cherry pie is always the first one I make, namely because that's all that stands between me and one spoonful after another of my favorite sweet-and-tart fruit wrapped in a flaky, buttery crust.

MAKES 6 TO 8 SERVINGS

2   pounds (910 g) pitted fresh or frozen sour cherries

1   cup (200 g) granulated sugar

¼   cup (30 g) cornstarch

2   teaspoons grated lime zest, (from about 2 limes)

3   tablespoons freshly squeezed lime juice (from about 2 limes)

¼   teaspoon salt

2   recipes Pie Dough (page 100)

1   large egg whisked with 1 teaspoon water

Turbinado sugar, for sprinkling

Directions

To make the filling, combine the cherries, sugar, cornstarch, lime zest and juice, and salt in a medium saucepan. Cook, stirring, over medium-low heat, until the mixture starts to bubble up and thicken. Remove from the heat and transfer the pie filling to the refrigerator to cool completely.

Once the filling has cooled, roll out one pie dough disk to ¼ inch/6 mm thick, placing it in a 9-inch/23 cm pie pan, leaving a 1-inch/2.5 cm overhang around the edge. Add the filling to the pastry-lined pie pan and transfer it to the refrigerator while the top crust is rolled out.

Roll out the remaining dough. Place the dough round on top of the pie and press the edges to seal, then flute the edge decoratively. Brush the entire pie with egg wash and sprinkle with turbinado sugar. Using a paring knife, cut four or five 1-inch/2.5 cm slits in the top of the pie dough.

Place the pie in the freezer to chill while the oven preheats to 375°F (190°C). Remove from the freezer. Set the pie pan on a baking sheet and bake until the crust is browned and the filling is bubbling, 50 to 55 minutes. Check the pie after 30 minutes and cover the top and edges with foil if they are becoming too dark. Remove from the oven and place on a wire rack to cool for at least 3 hours before serving.

MISSISSIPPI MUD PIE

The fact that this pie is as easy to make as it is good-looking secures its spot in the top ten desserts I make for almost any occasion. With its chocolate cookie crumble crust and thick, pudding-like chocolate filling, a little of this richly decadent pie goes a long way.

MAKES 6 TO 8 SERVINGS

1   (14.3-ounce/405 g) package chocolate sandwich cookies

1   cup (205 g) plus 1 tablespoon granulated sugar, divided

½   cup (113 g) unsalted butter, melted

2   cups (480 ml) whole milk

6   large egg yolks, at room temperature

3   tablespoons all-purpose flour

3   tablespoons unsweetened cocoa powder

10 ounces (285 g) bittersweet chocolate, chopped

1   tablespoon pure vanilla extract

2   cups (500 ml) heavy whipping cream

2   ounces (55 grams) bittersweet chocolate shavings

Directions

Preheat the oven to 350°F (180°C).

In a food processor, pulse the cookies until a fine crumb forms. Add 1 tablespoon of the sugar and the butter and pulse to combine. Gently press the remaining mixture into the bottom and sides of a 9-inch/23 cm pie pan.

Bake the crust for 8 to 10 minutes, or until set. Remove from the oven and place on a wire rack to cool completely.

In a medium saucepan over medium heat, bring the milk to a simmer. Set aside.

In a large bowl, whisk together the egg yolks, ¾ cup/ 150 g of the sugar, and the flour and cocoa powder. Whisking constantly, stream in the warm milk. Transfer the mixture to the saucepan used for the milk and bring to a boil over medium heat. Reduce the heat to medium-low and continue to cook, stirring constantly, until the back of a spoon drawn across the mixture leaves a trail, 1 to 2 minutes. Strain the mixture through a fine-mesh sieve and stir in the chopped chocolate and the vanilla. Pour the filling into the cookie crust and chill, uncovered, until the filling is firm and set, about 4 hours.

When ready to serve, in a large bowl, using an electric mixer on medium-high speed, beat the cream and the remaining ¼ cup/50 g of sugar until soft peaks form. Mound the whipped cream on top of the pie. Sprinkle the chocolate shavings on top of the whipped cream.

LONDON FOG BLUEBERRY HAND PIES

I never appreciated blueberries until I started baking with them. When you're making simple desserts with straightforward ingredients, you want to use the freshest produce possible. And when blueberries are at their peak seasonality in the summer, there's nothing more juicy, sweet, tart, and delicious. While the jammy blueberry filling for these hand pies could easily stand on its own, I take things one step further (of course!) by infusing it with subtly citrusy Earl Grey tea to complement the market-fresh flavor.

MAKES 12 HAND PIES

2   Earl Grey tea bags

⅓   cup (80 ml) boiling water

2   cups (320 g) blueberries, fresh or frozen

¼   cup (50 g) granulated sugar

3   tablespoons cornstarch

1   teaspoon vanilla bean paste

¼   teaspoon salt

2   recipes Pie Dough (page 100)

1   large egg

2   tablespoons turbinado sugar

TO MAKE THE FILLING: Add the tea bags to the boiling water and steep for 5 minutes. After 5 minutes, remove the tea bags and carefully squeeze them out into the tea. Combine the tea with the blueberries, granulated sugar, and cornstarch. Over medium heat, cook until the mixture starts to bubble and thicken, 5 to 7 minutes. Remove from the heat and set aside to cool to room temperature. Once cooled stir in vanilla bean paste and salt.

Roll out one pie dough disk to an 11-inch/28 cm circle that is ⅛ inch/3 mm thick. Trim the dough into an approximate 10-inch/25 cm square, then trim that into 4 squares, saving all the scraps.

Transfer the squares to a parchment-lined baking sheet and spoon a heaping tablespoon of filling onto one half of each of the squares. Fold the dough over and crimp the edges with a fork. Use a paring knife to make a small slit in the top of each pie. Repeat with the remaining pie dough, then repeat it once more by rolling out the dough scraps. Once all the pies are assembled, place the baking sheet in the freezer to chill while the oven preheats to 350°F (180°C).

Once the oven has preheated, beat the egg with 1 tablespoon of water and brush on top of the hand pies. Sprinkle with the turbinado sugar.

Bake until the crust is golden brown, 30 to 35 minutes. Remove from the oven and place on a wire rack to cool for 10 minutes, then serve warm or at room temperature.

BROWN BUTTER CHOCOLATE CHESS PIE

Chess pie—a sweet, custard-based staple of southern baking—is an ever-adaptable classic. For this version I punched up the classic with some chocolate and brown butter. It's a decadent combo that's just as delicious on its own as it is served warm with a scoop of ice cream.

MAKES 8 TO 10 SERVINGS

1   recipe Pie Dough (page 100)

¼   cup (55 g) unsalted butter

1   cup (200 g) granulated sugar

½   cup (45 g) unsweetened cocoa powder, sifted

⅓   cup (80 ml) whole milk

2   large eggs, at room temperature

1   teaspoon pure vanilla extract

¼   teaspoon salt

Directions

Preheat the oven to 350°F (180°C).

Roll out the pie dough to ¼ inch/6 mm thick and place in a 9-inch/23 cm pie pan, gently pressing the dough to the sides. Trim the edges leaving about 1 inch/2.5 cm of overhang, and create a fluted or crimped edge. Place a piece of parchment paper on top of the dough, add pie weights, and bake for 15 to 20 minutes, or until the dough is just turning golden brown. Remove from the oven. Remove the parchment paper and pie weights and let cool completely.

To make the filling, place the butter in a medium saucepan over medium heat and cook until the butter starts to bubble, brown, and smell nutty. Remove the pan from the heat, add the sugar, cocoa powder, and milk, and whisk until well combined and smooth. Add the eggs, vanilla, and salt and beat until just combined.

Pour the filling into the piecrust and transfer to the oven to bake for 30 to 35 minutes, or until the filling is just set and does not jiggle when the side of the pan is tapped. Tent the pie with foil if the edges become too brown. Remove from the oven and place on a wire rack to cool at room temperature for 2 to 3 hours before serving.

Pie Dough

This is a flexible pie dough that is strong and easy to handle. You should be able to drape it over your arm without its cracking, tearing, or stretching.

MAKES 1 (9-INCH/23 CM) SINGLE PIECRUST, EASILY DOUBLES FOR A DOUBLE CRUST

1½ cups (190 g) all-purpose flour, plus more for dusting

1 teaspoon granulated sugar

½ teaspoon salt

½ cup (113 g) unsalted butter, very cold and cut into ½-inch/ 1.3 cm cubes

⅓ cup (80 g) cold water

1 teaspoon cider vinegar

Ice cubes

Directions

In a food processor, pulse together the flour, sugar, and salt. Add the butter and give the mixture a 2-second pulse, 3 or 4 times, until the butter is the size of small peas. You may need more or less time, depending on your machine. Measure out the water in a measuring cup, then add the cider vinegar and enough ice to reach to ½ cup/125 ml measurement.

Add 2 tablespoons of the ice water mixture to the flour mixture and pulse a few times to incorporate. Continue adding the water mixture 1 tablespoon at a time, pulsing a couple of times after each addition. You should only need 1 or 2 more additional tablespoons. The mixture should look slightly dry, almost like a streusel topping.

Transfer the dough to a lightly floured work surface and form it into a 1-inch/2.5 cm-thick disk. Wrap in plastic wrap and refrigerate the dough for at least an hour, ideally overnight.

Tart Dough

This is a strong tart dough that easily rolls out and can be prepared ahead and stored covered in plastic wrap for up to two days before you need it.

MAKES 1 (9- OR 10-INCH/23 OR 25.5 CM) TART OR 6 (4-INCH/10 CM) TARTLETS

1⅔ cups (220 g) all-purpose flour, plus more for dusting

¼ cup (50 g) granulated sugar

¼ teaspoon salt

½ cup (113 g) unsalted butter, cold and cut into cubes

1 large egg, cold

Directions

In a food processor, pulse together the flour, sugar, and salt. Add the butter and pulse until the butter is the size of peas. Add the egg and pulse until the dough starts to come together. Transfer the dough to a floured work surface, pat into a ball, then flatten to a disk. Wrap the dough in plastic wrap and refrigerate for 1 hour.

To make a tart shell, roll out the dough to ¼ inch/6 mm thick and place it in the tart pan, carefully pressing it into the sides. Bake for 30 minutes at 350°F (180°C).

PLATE-SCRAPING CAKES

As I mentioned in the Introduction, I'm not a particularly linear thinker. Sensible order is really just a suggestion, especially when it comes to my baking adventures. When I first started out, my first foray, I successfully made the most perfect batch of cookies. So, it only made sense that for my next trick, I'd make a cake . . . for advanced bakers. It was a monumental flop. Delicious, but not exactly showcase-worthy. After that, I went on to learn the basics: the difference between baking powder and baking soda, and the role of eggs in cake. After that, cakes were, well, a piece of cake! They continue to be my favorite things to make (and eat). Sure, I still get frustrated at times with less-than-perfect finishes, but let's make a pact that we are going to embrace any messy pipings, uneven drizzles, and deflated layers; be proud of them; and devour every last crumb.

BANANA UPSIDE-DOWN CAKE

Anyone who has had upside-down cake knows that the caramelized-sugar crust on top is everything. This syrupy, chewy sweetness is what sets apart a great upside-down cake from the rest, and is why this updated version of a vintage classic involves taking a kitchen torch to the top of the cake after it bakes—just to make sure that you're in good crust business. And in the spirit of updates, I've also swapped out pineapples for bananas and soaked the whole thing in rum.

MAKES 6 TO 8 SERVINGS

Nonstick cooking spray

For the topping

¼ cup (55 g) unsalted butter

¼ cup (50 g) light brown sugar

3 tablespoons dark rum

3 large bananas, just ripe, halved lengthwise

For the batter

1½ cups (200 g) all-purpose flour

1½ teaspoons baking powder

½ teaspoon salt

6 tablespoons (85 g) unsalted butter, at room temperature

1 cup (200 g) granulated sugar

1 large egg, at room temperature

1 tablespoon dark rum

1 teaspoon pure vanilla extract

1 cup (250 ml) buttermilk

Directions

Preheat the oven to 350°F (180°C). Lightly cover a 13 x 9-inch/33 x 23 cm baking pan with nonstick cooking spray.

TO MAKE THE TOPPING: In a small sauté pan over medium heat, melt the butter and brown sugar together, stirring to incorporate. Add the rum.

Pour the butter mixture into the bottom of the prepared pan and spread evenly. Carefully place the banana halves, flat side down, in the pan and set aside.

TO MAKE THE BATTER: In a medium bowl, whisk together the flour, baking powder, and salt. Set aside. In a large bowl, using an electric mixer, cream together the butter and granulated sugar until light and fluffy, 4 to 6 minutes. Beat in the egg, then the rum and vanilla. Beating on low speed, starting and ending with the flour mixture, alternate adding the flour mixture and the buttermilk. Mix until only just combined.

Carefully pour and spread the batter over the bananas. Bake for 35 to 40 minutes, or until a toothpick inserted into the center comes out clean. Remove from the oven. Let the cake rest in its pan for 10 minutes on a wire rack, then carefully flip over. Using a kitchen torch, brown the tops of the bananas.

BLACK FOREST CRÊPE CAKE

This impressive cake is a labor of love. It's layers upon layers of dainty chocolate crêpes piled high with white chocolate ganache and cherry filling, topped with whipped cream, and dotted with fresh cherries. With a little planning, you can easily pull off this patisserie-worthy dessert. Simply make the crêpe batter and fillings up to two days in advance, and then assemble the cake on the day you plan to serve.

MAKES 8 TO 10 SERVINGS

For the chocolate crêpes

2   large eggs, at room temperature

1   cup (225 ml) whole milk

⅔   cup (80 g) all-purpose flour

3   tablespoons unsweetened cocoa powder

1   teaspoon instant espresso powder

2   tablespoons unsalted butter, melted

½   teaspoon pure vanilla extract

¼   cup (50 g) granulated sugar

    Nonstick cooking spray

For the cherry filling

2   cups (480 ml) red wine

1   cup (200 g) granulated sugar

    Grated zest of 1 lemon

2   cinnamon sticks

2   cardamom pods, lightly crushed

2   pounds (907 g) fresh cherries, pitted

2   teaspoons pure vanilla extract

(ingredients continue)

For the white chocolate ganache

1   pound (453 g) white chocolate, roughly chopped

2½   cups (591 ml) heavy whipping cream

For the garnish

1   cup (240 ml) heavy whipping cream

2   tablespoons confectioners' sugar

1   cup (225 g) fresh cherries

1   tablespoon semisweet or bittersweet chocolate shavings

Directions

TO MAKE THE CRÊPES: In a blender, combine the eggs, milk, flour, cocoa powder, espresso powder, melted butter, vanilla, and granulated sugar. Blend on high speed until the mixture is well combined, about 30 seconds. Cover and refrigerate the batter for 1 hour or up to 2 days.

Line a large baking sheet with parchment paper.

Lightly coat a crêpe pan or 8-inch/20.5 cm nonstick skillet with nonstick cooking spray. Heat the pan over medium heat until hot. Remove from the heat and coat the bottom of the still-hot pan with 2 tablespoons of the crêpe batter, tilting the pan for even distribution. Return the pan to medium heat and cook until the crêpe is dry to the touch and matte in appearance, 1 to 2 minutes. Carefully flip the crêpe over, using a spatula, and cook for another 15 to 30 seconds. Invert the pan over the baking sheet to release the crêpe and cover the crêpe with a piece of parchment paper.

Lightly coat the pan again and repeat with the remaining batter, layering parchment paper atop each finished crêpe. Let the crêpes cool to room temperature.

TO MAKE THE CHERRY FILLING: In a medium saucepan over medium-high heat, bring the wine, granulated sugar, lemon zest, cinnamon sticks, and cardamom pods to a boil. Add the cherries and lower the heat to medium-low. Simmer the cherries for about 10 minutes, or until the liquid is reduced by half. Remove the mixture from the heat and stir in the vanilla. Set aside to cool completely.

TO MAKE THE WHITE CHOCOLATE GANACHE: Place the white chocolate in a large, heatproof bowl and set aside. In a medium saucepan, heat the cream over medium heat until it barely simmers. Pour the warm cream over the chocolate and let it sit for 5 minutes before incorporating the chocolate.

Whisk until completely smooth. Cover the bowl and refrigerate for 2 hours, or until well chilled. Using an electric mixer, beat on high speed for 1 to 2 minutes, or until light and fluffy. Do not overmix, or the mixture will start to look almost curdled and almost dry.

Assemble the crêpe cake by laying 1 crêpe on a serving platter. Spread 3 to 4 tablespoons of the white chocolate ganache evenly over the crêpe. Top with 2 to 3 tablespoons of the cherry filling and another crêpe. Repeat with the remaining crêpes, white chocolate ganache, and cherry filling.

FOR THE GARNISH: In a bowl, using an electric mixer on medium-high speed, whip the cream and confectioners' sugar together until soft peaks form. Top the crêpe cake with the whipped cream, cherries, and chocolate shavings.

CHOCOLATE AFFOGATO MOUSSE CAKE

This cake will please all the coffee lovers, chocolate lovers, and everyone else in between. Its lightly fluffy texture makes it the perfect after-dinner dessert when you want something light, but don't want to miss out on any flavor or richness.

MAKES 8 TO 10 SERVINGS

Nonstick cooking spray

For the cheesecake

2 (8-ounce/452 g) packages cream cheese

⅓ cup (70 g) granulated sugar

2 large eggs, at room temperature

3 tablespoons pure vanilla extract

For the crust

5 cups (311 g) whole chocolate wafer cookies, plus more for garnish

½ cup (113 g) unsalted butter, melted

For the mousse

8 large egg yolks, at room temperature

½ cup (100 g) granulated sugar

¼ cup (60 ml) light corn syrup

10 ounces (285 g) bittersweet chocolate, melted and cooled slightly

2½ teaspoons instant espresso powder

2 teaspoons pure vanilla extract

½ teaspoon salt

2 cups (480 ml) heavy whipping cream

2 tablespoons confectioners' sugar

4 large egg whites, at room temperature

(ingredients continue)

Directions

Preheat the oven to 375°F (190°C). Spray a 9-inch/23 cm springform pan, 9-inch/23 cm round cake pan, or other similar dish with nonstick cooking spray, to bake the cheesecake.

TO MAKE THE CHEESECAKE: In a large bowl, using an electric mixer, mix the cream cheese, granulated sugar, eggs, and vanilla until smooth. Pour the mixture into the 9-inch/23 cm pan. Bake for 20 to 25 minutes, or until the center is set. Transfer to a wire rack to cool completely. Once cooled, cover and chill completely for at least 2 hours or overnight. The cheesecake can be prepared 3 days ahead and kept covered and refrigerated. Don't worry if there are cracks in the top, as you'll be scooping it out into another pan.

TO MAKE THE CRUST: In a food processor, pulse the cookies until a fine crumb forms. Add the melted butter and pulse for another 30 seconds. Spray a second 9-inch/23 cm springform pan with nonstick cooking spray and press the mixture into the prepared pan.

Remove the cheesecake from the refrigerator. Scoop and roll the mixture into 1½-inch/4 cm balls. Gently place and push the cheesecake balls onto the crust, maintaining their shape. Place the pan in the freezer to keep cold while you make the chocolate mousse.

TO MAKE THE MOUSSE: In a large bowl, using an electric mixer on medium speed, beat the egg yolks until pale and frothy, 4 to 5 minutes. Meanwhile, in a saucepan, combine the granulated sugar, corn syrup, and 2 tablespoons of water and bring to a boil over medium-high heat. Cook for 1 to 3 minutes, or until a candy thermometer reads 245°F (118°C).

Beating on low speed, slowly and carefully stream the sugar mixture into the egg yolk mixture. Increase the speed to medium and mix until thickened, 2 to 3 minutes. Beat in the melted chocolate, espresso powder, vanilla, and salt. Set aside.

In a separate bowl, using clean beaters, beat the cream and confectioners' sugar on medium-high speed until soft peaks form.

Fold 1 cup/235 ml of the whipped cream into the chocolate mixture, then add the remaining whipped cream. Pour the chocolate mousse on top of the cheesecake balls and rap the pan against the countertop, to settle the mousse. Use an offset spatula to smooth the top to an even finish, and refrigerate until set, at least 4 hours.

SMASHED BERRY LEMON POPPY SEED BUNDT CAKE

This berry-stained cake doesn't require any decoration, which makes it ideal when you want a no-fuss dessert.

MAKES 8 TO 10 SERVINGS

For the smashed berry filling

- ½ cup (80 g) fresh or frozen blueberries
- ½ cup (80 g) fresh or frozen blackberries
- 3 tablespoons granulated sugar
- 1½ tablespoons freshly squeezed lemon juice
- 1 tablespoon cornstarch

For the cake

- Unsalted butter, for pan
- 2½ cups (300 g) all-purpose flour
- 1¾ cups (350 g) granulated sugar
- 1 teaspoon baking powder
- 1 teaspoon baking soda
- ½ teaspoon salt
- ⅔ cup (170 ml) vegetable oil
- ½ cup (130 ml) buttermilk
- 2 tablespoons lemon zest
- ¼ cup (60 ml) freshly squeezed lemon juice
- 3 large eggs, at room temperature
- 2 tablespoons poppy seeds

Directions

TO MAKE THE SMASHED BERRY FILLING:
Combine all the filling ingredients in a medium saucepan over medium heat. Cook, smashing the berries, until the mixture starts to bubble and thicken, 2 to 3 minutes. Set the mixture aside to cool to room temperature.

Preheat the oven to 350°F (180°C). Lightly butter and flour a 10-cup/2.4 L Bundt pan.

TO MAKE THE CAKE: Whisk together the flour, sugar, baking powder, baking soda, and salt in a large bowl. In a second bowl, beat together the oil, buttermilk, lemon zest and juice, and eggs until well combined. Stir the wet ingredients into the dry ingredients until just combined. Fold in the poppy seeds.

Pour half of the batter into the prepared pan and layer with half of the filling. Repeat with the remaining batter and filling. Bake for 40 to 45 minutes, or until the cake turns golden brown and a toothpick inserted into the center comes out clean. Transfer to a wire rack and let cool for 30 to 40 minutes before inverting the pan to release the cake.

CARAMEL, PEAR, and WALNUT CAKE with CRÈME FRAÎCHE WHIPPED CREAM

There's something so elegant about the warm, spiced flavors of fall, especially with sophisticated slices of pear draped across the top. But make no mistake: this deceptively refined cake is no-nonsense at heart.

MAKES 6 TO 8 SERVINGS

Nonstick cooking spray

For the cake

2 cups (240 g) all-purpose flour

2 teaspoons baking powder

½ teaspoon ground allspice

½ teaspoon ground cinnamon

½ teaspoon ground ginger

¼ teaspoon salt

¾ cup (170 g) unsalted butter, at room temperature

1 cup (215 g) packed light brown sugar

3 large eggs, at room temperature

1 teaspoon pure vanilla extract

¾ cup (180 ml) buttermilk

1 cup (120 g) walnuts, toasted and chopped

3 pears (about 1 pound/453 g), peeled, cored, and diced in 1-inch/2.5 cm pieces

For the caramel

1 cup (200 g) granulated sugar

1½ cups (355 ml) heavy whipping cream

½ teaspoon sea salt

(ingredients continue)

For the crème fraîche whipped cream

1½ cups (355 ml) heavy whipping cream

½ cup (115 g) crème fraîche

Directions

Preheat the oven to 350°F (180°C). Line the bottom of a 9-inch/23 cm round cake pan with parchment paper and spray the sides with nonstick cooking spray.

TO MAKE THE CAKE: In a medium bowl, combine the flour, baking powder, allspice, cinnamon, ginger, and salt. Set aside.

In a large bowl, using an electric mixer on medium speed, cream the butter and brown sugar until light and fluffy, 3 to 5 minutes. Beat in the eggs, 1 at a time, then the vanilla. Beating on low speed, starting and ending with the flour mixture, alternate adding the flour mixture and buttermilk until combined. Fold in the walnuts and pears. Pour the batter into the prepared pan and bake for 35 to 40 minutes, or until a toothpick inserted into the center comes out clean. Remove from the oven and place the pan on a wire rack to cool.

TO MAKE THE CARAMEL: Combine the granulated sugar and 2 tablespoons of water in a medium saucepan over medium-high heat. Bring to a boil and cook, not stirring, until the mixture turns a light amber color, 4 to 6 minutes. Remove from the heat, carefully pour in the cream and salt, and whisk to incorporate. If the caramel seizes up, return the pan to the stovetop over low and whisk until the cream is incorporated. Let cool for 10 to 15 minutes.

WHEN READY TO ASSEMBLE THE CAKE, MAKE THE CRÈME FRAÎCHE WHIPPED CREAM: In a bowl, using an electric mixer on medium-high speed, beat the cream and crème fraîche until soft peaks form.

Spread the caramel sauce over the cake, letting the caramel drizzle down the sides, then place a large dollop of crème fraîche whipped cream on top. Serve immediately.

BANANA CUPCAKES
with MAPLE PECAN FROSTING

This cupcake might not win any beauty contests (brown frosting wouldn't stand a chance next to all the pretty pastels in the world), but the rich, complex maple-pecan mash-up more than makes up for looks in flavor.

MAKES 24 CUPCAKES

For the cupcakes

- 3 cups (360 g) cake flour
- 1 teaspoon baking powder
- 1 teaspoon baking soda
- ½ teaspoon salt
- ½ cup (115 ml) buttermilk
- ¼ cup (50 ml) vegetable oil
- 2 teaspoons pure vanilla extract
- ½ cup (113 g) unsalted butter, at room temperature
- 1 cup (200 g) granulated sugar
- ¼ cup (55 g) lightly packed dark brown sugar
- 1 cup (230 g) mashed banana (from about 3 medium bananas)
- 2 large egg yolks
- 1 large egg

For the frosting

- ¾ cup (85 g) finely chopped pecans
- 4 ounces (115 g) cream cheese, at room temperature
- 1 cup (225 g) unsalted butter, at room temperature
- 1 cup (215 g) packed dark brown sugar
- ¼ cup (80 g) pure maple syrup
- 1 teaspoon pure vanilla extract
- ½ teaspoon kosher salt
- 2 cups (240 g) confectioners' sugar

Directions

Preheat the oven to 350°F (180°C). Arrange racks in the upper and lower thirds of the oven. Line 24 standard muffin cups with paper liners.

TO MAKE THE CUPCAKES: In a large bowl, whisk together the cake flour, baking powder, baking soda, and salt. In a medium bowl, stir together the butter-milk, oil, and vanilla.

In a separate large bowl, using an electric mixer on medium speed, cream together the butter, granulated sugar, brown sugar, and mashed bananas, 3 to 5 minutes. Add the yolks, 1 at a time, then the egg, beating after each addition until well combined and occasionally scraping down the sides and bottom of the bowl. Continue to beat until the mixture turns airy and pale yellow, 2 to 3 minutes.

Beating on low speed, starting and ending with the flour mixture, alternate adding the flour mixture and buttermilk mixture in 3 additions. Divide the batter among the paper-lined muffin cups. Rotating the pans from left to right and top to bottom halfway through, bake for 18 to 20 minutes, until the tops are light golden brown and a toothpick inserted into the center of a cupcake comes out clean. Remove from the oven and place the pans on wire racks to cool completely. Leave the oven on.

TO MAKE THE FROSTING: Spread the pecans onto a baking sheet and toast until browned, 5 to 7 minutes. Remove from the oven and allow to cool completely.

In a large bowl, combine the cream cheese, butter, brown sugar, maple syrup, vanilla, and salt. Using an electric mixer on medium speed, beat until light and fluffy, 2 to 3 minutes. Gradually add the confectioners' sugar, ½ cup/60 g at a time, beating well after each addition. Add the cooled pecans and beat until well combined. Pipe or spread the frosting on the cooled cupcakes.

RASPBERRY ALMOND OPERA CAKE

I have always been a huge fan of opera cake, so when I set out to riff on it, I made raspberries the star. This is a multistep recipe, so do yourself a favor and make all the components ahead and assemble it the next day. You can short-cut the recipe by using a high-quality raspberry jam instead of making it from scratch.

MAKES 1 (6 X 7.5-INCH/15 X 19 CM) LAYER CAKE

Nonstick cooking spray

Unsalted butter, for pan

For the almond sponge cake

6   large egg whites, at room temperature

½   teaspoon cream of tartar

¾   cup (150 g) granulated sugar, divided

2   cups (190 g) almond flour

⅔   cup (85 g) all-purpose flour

½   teaspoon baking powder

6   large eggs, at room temperature

2   cups (240 g) confectioners' sugar

3   tablespoons unsalted butter, melted and cooled slightly

1   teaspoon pure vanilla extract

For the raspberry jam

18 ounces (510 g) fresh or frozen raspberries

½   cup (100 g) granulated sugar

1   (1.2-ounce/34-g) package freeze-dried raspberries, crushed to a fine crumb

For the buttercream

5   large egg whites, at room temperature

1½ cups (300 g) granulated sugar

2   cups (455 g) unsalted butter, at room temperature, cut into 1-tablespoon pieces

¼   cup (65 g) raspberry jam

1½ teaspoons pure vanilla extract

Gold dragées, for garnish (optional)

Directions

Preheat the oven to 425°F (220°C). Lightly coat two 18 x 13-inch/45.5 x 33 cm rimmed baking sheets with nonstick cooking spray. Press and flatten parchment on top. Lightly brush the top of the parchment paper with butter.

TO MAKE THE ALMOND SPONGE CAKE: In a large bowl, beat the egg whites on low speed until frothy. Add the cream of tartar and increase the speed to high. Gradually add ¼ cup (50 g) of the granulated sugar while continuing to beat the mixture until soft peaks form.

In a medium bowl, sift together the almond flour, all-purpose flour, and baking powder. Set aside.

In a separate large bowl, beat the eggs, confectioners' sugar, and remaining ½ cup (100 g) of granulated sugar until light and fluffy and, when the beaters are lifted, the mixture falls into a ribbon, 3 to 5 minutes. Fold in the almond flour mixture.

Fold the egg whites into the almond flour mixture, then gently fold in the melted butter and vanilla. Pour the batter onto the prepared baking sheets. Bake until barely golden brown, 8 to 10 minutes. Remove from the oven and

place the pans on a wire rack to cool completely. The sponge cake can be made up to 3 days in advance. Cover with plastic wrap and keep refrigerated.

TO MAKE THE RASPBERRY JAM: In a large saucepan, combine the jam ingredients. Bring to a boil over medium-high heat, then lower the heat and let the mixture simmer for 8 to 10 minutes, until reduced by one quarter. Remove from the heat and set aside to cool completely. The jam can be made up to 3 days in advance and kept tightly covered and refrigerated.

TO MAKE THE BUTTERCREAM: Place the egg whites and granulated sugar in a large, heatproof bowl. Place the bowl over a pan of simmering water (do not let the bottom of the bowl touch the water). Cook, stirring, until the mixture reaches 160°F (71°C). Remove the bowl from the heat and beat the mixture on high speed with an electric mixer until it is just barely warm. Add the butter 1 tablespoon at a time, beating until completely combined before adding another. (If the butter starts to melt, stop adding the butter and beat the

(directions continue)

127

PLATE-SCRAPING CAKES

mixture some more to cool it further.) When all the butter has been incorporated, measure out 1½ cups of frosting. Place measured out frosting in a bowl and add ¼ cup (63 g) of the raspberry jam and beat until well combined. Add the vanilla to the remaining buttercream and beat until well combined.

TO ASSEMBLE THE CAKE: Cut each sponge cake in half through the long edge to form 4 equal rectangles (6 x 7.5 inches/15 x 19 cm). Place 1 rectangle on a serving platter. Divide the remaining raspberry jam into thirds; do the same for the raspberry buttercream.

Top the bottom cake layer with raspberry buttercream, spreading evenly. Top with raspberry jam, spreading evenly, then top with another layer of cake. Repeat this process—a layer of cake, then raspberry buttercream, raspberry jam—once more, then add the final layer of cake. On top of the final layer, spread a thin layer of the vanilla buttercream. Place the rest in a pastry bag fitted with a Wilton #104 tip and top with a braided pattern by piping a small slanted line at a 45-degree angle to just past an imaginary center line. Go to the right and pipe just past the center and over the end of the bottom left line. Repeat and a braid will appear. Use a serrated knife to carefully trim and even up the edges, as needed. Sprinkle gold dragées on top, if using.

FUNNEL CAKE CUPCAKES

These whimsical cupcakes disappear more quickly than any other cupcake I make. The Funnel Cake Bites toppers (page 192) give them a nostalgic feel that brings people back to summers at the state fair.

MAKES 24 CUPCAKES

For the cupcakes

- 2½ cups (300 g) all-purpose flour
- 1 tablespoon baking powder
- 1 tablespoon ground cinnamon
- ½ teaspoon salt
- ¾ cup (170 g) unsalted butter, at room temperature
- 1 cup (200 g) granulated sugar
- 4 large eggs, at room temperature
- 1 teaspoon pure vanilla extract
- 1 cup (240 ml) whole milk

For the buttercream

- 6 cups (720 g) confectioners' sugar
- ¾ cup (170 g) unsalted butter, at room temperature
- 3 tablespoons milk, plus more if needed
- 2 teaspoons pure vanilla extract
- ¼ teaspoon salt

Cinnamon and Sugar Funnel Cake Bites (page 192)

Directions

Preheat the oven to 350°F (180°C). Line two 12-cup muffin tin with foil or paper liners.

TO MAKE THE CUPCAKES: In a small bowl, whisk together the flour, baking powder, cinnamon, and salt. Set aside.

In a large bowl, using an electric mixer on medium speed, cream the butter and granulated sugar together until light and fluffy, 2 to 3 minutes. On low speed, beat in the eggs, 1 at a time, followed by the vanilla. Beating on low speed, starting and ending with the flour, alternately add the flour and milk, beating just until combined.

Divide the batter among the prepared muffin cups, filling each about three quarters of the way full. Bake until golden on top and a toothpick inserted into the center of a cupcake comes out clean, 18 to 20 minutes.

Remove from the oven and allow the cupcakes to cool in the muffin tin for 5 minutes, then transfer to a wire rack to cool completely.

WHEN READY TO ASSEMBLE THE CUPCAKES, MAKE THE BUTTER-CREAM: In a bowl, combine the confectioners' sugar, butter, milk, vanilla, and salt. Using an electric mixer on high speed, beat until light and fluffy. If the frosting is dry, add 1 teaspoon of milk at a time to reach the desired consistency.

Assemble the cupcakes by spreading the frosting on top of the cupcakes, then topping with the cooled funnel cake bites.

MOLASSES BUNDT CAKE
with BOURBON CARAMEL SAUCE

Judging by appearances, this cake is no head-turner. But once you discover the complex, deep, rich flavor of molasses and how it plays off the bourbon caramel, there'll be no greater beauty in your mind.

MAKES 8 TO 10 SERVINGS

Unsalted butter, for pan

For the cake

3½ cups (420 g) all-purpose flour, plus more for pan

1¼ cups (250 g) granulated sugar

2 teaspoons ground ginger

2 teaspoons ground cinnamon

½ teaspoon ground allspice

½ teaspoon ground cardamom

½ teaspoon freshly ground black pepper

1 teaspoon salt

1 teaspoon baking soda

1 teaspoon baking powder

1 cup (250 ml) vegetable oil

1 cup (250 ml) molasses

1 cup (250 ml) brewed black coffee, at room temperature

3 large eggs, at room temperature

2 teaspoons pure vanilla extract

For the bourbon caramel sauce

1 cup (200 g) granulated sugar

½ cup (120 ml) heavy whipping cream

2 tablespoons unsalted butter

¼ cup (60 ml) bourbon

Pinch of sea salt

Directions

Preheat the oven to 350°F (180°C). Lightly butter and flour a 10-cup (2.4 L) Bundt pan.

TO MAKE THE CAKE: In a large bowl, whisk together the flour, sugar, ginger, cinnamon, allspice, cardamom, pepper, salt, baking soda, and baking powder. In a second bowl, using an electric mixer on medium speed, beat together the oil, molasses, coffee, eggs, and vanilla. Stir the wet ingredients into the dry ingredients, mixing until just combined.

Pour the batter into the prepared pan. Bake for 35 to 40 minutes, or until a toothpick inserted into the center comes out clean. Transfer to a wire rack to cool for 30 to 40 minutes before inverting the pan to release the cake.

TO MAKE THE BOURBON CARAMEL SAUCE: Place the sugar and ¼ cup (60 ml) of water in a small saucepan. Cook, stirring, over medium-high heat until the sugar is dissolved. Use a pastry brush to wash down any sugar crystals from the sides of the pot. Bring to a boil, about 3 minutes. Once boiling, do not stir directly. Instead, using the long handle of the pot, tilt and swirl the mixture to distribute the heat evenly. At 7 to 8 minutes, the color will start to change. Watch the mixture closely and continue to tilt and swirl the pan to even out the color. Continue to cook and swirl until the mixture is a dark amber, 1 to 2 minutes after you see the first amber color. Remove from the heat immediately. Add the cream carefully, as it will bubble and splatter. Add the butter and stir until fully dissolved. Stir in the bourbon and salt. The caramel can be made 1 week ahead and kept covered and refrigerated.

To assemble, drizzle the caramel sauce on top of the cake.

CANNOLI CAKEIFTS

Like many, I don't love deep-frying. If there is a shortcut to be had, I'm going to use it. It always seems rather tedious to me to take the extra steps in wrapping the dough on a form, sealing it, holding it in the hot oil, then slipping it off the form—it's a lot to do for one little shell. So, most times when I make cannoli, I go for the deconstructed version using baked wonton wrappers. Skip the forms and bake the dough cutouts, layer them up with sweet, creamy filling, and call it a cannoli cakelet. Just make sure the ricotta and cream cheese are the same temperature, to ensure you get the smoothest filling.

MAKES 6 SERVINGS

16 ounces (450 g) whole-milk ricotta

4 ounces (110 g) cream cheese, at room temperature

½ cup (60 g) confectioners' sugar

½ teaspoon pure vanilla extract

18 wonton wrappers

2 tablespoons unsalted butter, melted

2 tablespoons granulated sugar

3½ ounces (100 g) semisweet chocolate, chopped

¼ cup (40 g) shelled pistachios, finely chopped

Preheat the oven to 350°F (180°C). Line 2 baking sheets with parchment paper.

In a food processor, place the ricotta, cream cheese, confectioners' sugar, and vanilla. Pulse to combine, then scrape down sides. Process the mixture until smooth and creamy, about 30 seconds. Transfer the mixture to the refrigerator to chill and set while you make the cannoli shells.

To make the cannoli shells, stamp out rounds from the wonton wrappers with a 3-inch/7.5 cm biscuit cutter. Place the rounds on the prepared baking sheets and brush one side with melted butter. Sprinkle lightly with granulated sugar, then flip over and repeat with the remaining butter and sugar. Bake until lightly golden, 6 to 8 minutes. Remove from the oven and transfer the baking sheets to a wire rack to the let the shells cool completely.

Once the cannoli rounds are completely cool, place the chopped chocolate in a bowl set over a small pot of barely simmering water, making sure the bottom of the bowl isn't touching the water, and gently stir until melted. Alternatively, in a microwave-safe bowl, melt the chocolate in a microwave on MEDIUM-HIGH in 30-second bursts, stirring between each burst. Dip the edge of the shell all the way around and rim with pistachios. Place the finished shell on a clean parchment sheet to set. Repeat with the remaining shells.

When ready to serve, transfer the chilled filling to a pastry bag fitted with Wilton's 1M tip. Lay 1 cannoli round on a serving platter. Pipe 2 tablespoons of filling on top. Top with an additional cannoli round and 2 tablespoons of filling; finish with 1 more cannoli round. Repeat with the remaining ingredients until all the cakelets are assembled. Serve immediately.

CHERRY ALMOND CAKE

If there were one cake I could eat every day, this would be it—not too sweet, not too dense: just right. The only thing that saves me from cutting myself a slice of this every day is the short cherry season. To get the best results, Bing or Dark Hudson cherries are my first choices; of course, you will still have a tasty cake no matter what cherry variety you can source.

MAKES 8 TO 10 SERVINGS

Nonstick cooking spray

1 cup (130 g) cake flour

1½ teaspoons baking powder

¼ teaspoon salt

¾ cup (150 g) granulated sugar

7 ounces (200 g) almond paste, broken into 1-inch/2.5 cm pieces

¾ cup (170 g) unsalted butter, at room temperature

4 large eggs, at room temperature

2 teaspoons dark rum

1 teaspoon almond extract

1½ pounds (600 g) frozen cherries

1 tablespoon all-purpose flour

3 to 4 tablespoons sliced almonds, or as needed

Confectioners' sugar, for dusting

Directions

Preheat the oven to 350°F (180°C). Spray a 9-inch/23 cm tube pan with nonstick cooking spray.

In a small bowl, sift together the cake flour, baking powder, and salt. Set aside.

In the bowl of a food processor, pulse the granulated sugar and almond paste until the mixture resembles wet sand.

In a bowl, using an electric mixer on medium speed, cream together the butter and almond paste mixture until light and fluffy, 3 to 5 minutes. Beat in the eggs, 1 at a time, followed by the rum and almond extract. Add the cake flour mixture and mix on low speed until just combined. Set aside. In a separate bowl, toss the cherries in the all-purpose flour.

Spoon the batter into the prepared pan and sprinkle the cherries on top, pressing gently so the fruit sinks slightly into the batter.

Bake until golden brown, 55 to 60 minutes, or until a toothpick inserted into the center comes out clean. Remove from the oven and allow to cool for 10 minutes in the pan on a wire rack. Carefully invert the pan to release the cake. Sprinkle the top with almonds and dust with confectioners' sugar.

STRAWBERRY and LEMON CREAM COCONUT CAKE

This cake always reminds me of summer with its bright red strawberry crown. Every May when strawberry season starts, Matt and I make an effort to take the boys strawberry picking, something he fondly remembers doing as a kid. We don't always make it, but I do always manage to celebrate the season with this cake.

MAKES 8 TO 10 SERVINGS

For the cake

4 cups (180 g) all purpose flour

2 teaspoons baking powder

1½ teaspoons baking soda

1½ teaspoons salt

1½ cups (354 ml) buttermilk

½ cup (120 ml) vegetable oil

2 teaspoons pure vanilla extract

2 teaspoons pure coconut extract

1 cup (225 g) unsalted butter, at room temperature

2¼ cups (950 g) granulated sugar

4 large eggs, at room temperature

(ingredients continue)

For the buttercream frosting

- 6 cups (681 g) confectioners' sugar
- ¾ cup (170 g) unsalted butter, at room temperature
- 2 tablespoons milk, plus more if needed
- 2 teaspoons pure vanilla extract
- 1 tablespoon lemon zest
- 2 tablespoons freshly squeezed lemon juice
- ¼ teaspoon salt

For the garnish

- ¼ cup (25 g) sweetened coconut flakes, toasted
- 1 cup (167 g) strawberries, hulled and sliced

Directions

Preheat the oven to 350°F (180°C). Line three 8-inch/20.5 cm round baking pans with parchment paper.

TO MAKE THE CAKE: In a large bowl, combine the flour, baking powder, baking soda, and salt. Set aside.

In a medium bowl, whisk together the buttermilk, vegetable oil, and vanilla and coconut extracts. Set aside.

In a bowl, using an electric mixer on medium speed, cream together the butter and 2 cups/400 g of the granulated sugar until light and fluffy, 3 to 5 minutes. Beat in the eggs, 1 at a time. Beating on low speed, starting and ending with the flour mixture, alternate adding the flour mixture and the buttermilk mixture in 3 additions.

Divide the batter evenly among the 3 prepared cake pans and bake until a toothpick inserted into the center comes out clean, 35 to 40 minutes. Remove from the oven and transfer the pans to wire racks to cool completely.

WHEN READY TO ASSEMBLE THE CAKE, MAKE THE BUTTERCREAM FROSTING: In a bowl, combine the confectioners' sugar, butter, milk, vanilla, lemon zest and juice, and salt. Using an electric mixer on medium speed, beat until light and fluffy, 2 to 3 minutes, scraping the side of the bowl. If the frosting is dry, add 1 additional teaspoon of milk at a time to reach the desired consistency.

Assemble the cake by placing 1 cake layer on a serving platter. Spread ½ cup/120 ml of the buttercream on top. Add a second cake layer and spread ½ cup/120 ml of the buttercream on top. Top with the remaining cake layer and spread the remaining buttercream over the top and sides of the cake. Press coconut flakes into the side of cake all the way around. Finish by sprinkling coconut flakes on top of the cake and top with the strawberries.

FRENCH SILK CRUNCH CAKE

As I was learning to bake, I rarely passed up trying new chocolate cake recipes. And over the years, I've probably made more chocolate cakes than any other dessert. Of all of them, though, this recipe is the one I return to again and again. The cake is rich, dark, and moist—as a chocolate cake should be!—but what takes it from afternoon teacake to an event-worthy layered masterpiece is the crunchy chocolate candy studded throughout.

MAKES 6 SERVINGS

For the cake

- 1⅓ cups (270 g) granulated sugar
- 1¼ cups (150 g) all-purpose flour
- ¾ cup (70 g) unsweetened cocoa powder, sifted
- 1 teaspoon baking soda
- ½ teaspoon salt
- 1 cup (240 ml) buttermilk
- ½ cup (120 ml) vegetable oil
- 3 large eggs
- 1 teaspoon pure vanilla extract

For the crunch

- 6 ounces (170 g) semisweet chocolate, roughly chopped
- 1¼ cups (33 g) crispy rice cereal

For the chocolate buttercream

- 6 ounces (170 g) unsweetened chocolate, roughly chopped
- 4 cups (480 g) confectioners' sugar
- ¾ cup (170 g) unsalted butter, at room temperature
- 3 tablespoons whole milk, plus more if needed
- 2 teaspoons pure vanilla extract
- ¼ teaspoon salt

Directions

Preheat the oven to 350°F (180°C). Line three 6-inch/15 cm cake pans with parchment paper.

TO MAKE THE CAKE: In a large bowl, whisk together the sugar, flour, cocoa powder, baking soda, and salt. Set aside.

In a large measuring cup, measure the buttermilk, then pour the vegetable oil into the same cup. Add the eggs and vanilla and beat together with a fork. Add to the dry mixture and whisk until the batter comes together.

Evenly divide the cake mixture among the prepared pans and bake for 20 to 25 minutes, or until a toothpick inserted into the center of a cake comes out clean. Remove from the oven and place the pans on a wire rack to cool for 1 hour. Carefully remove the cake from the pans and let cool completely.

IN THE MEANTIME, MAKE THE CRUNCH: Line a baking sheet with parchment paper and set aside. In a microwave-safe bowl, melt the chocolate in a microwave on MEDIUM-HIGH in 5-second bursts, stirring between bursts, until the chocolate is fully melted (or melt in a double boiler). Add the crispy rice cereal and stir to coat, then spread the mixture on a parchment-lined baking sheet. Transfer the crunch to the refrigerator to chill and set.

TO MAKE THE CHOCOLATE BUTTERCREAM: In a microwave-safe bowl, melt the chocolate in a microwave on MEDIUM-HIGH in 5-second bursts, stirring between bursts until the chocolate is fully melted (or melt in a double boiler). Set aside to cool to room temperature.

In a large bowl, combine the confectioners' sugar, butter, milk, vanilla, and salt. Using an electric mixer, beat on medium speed until light and fluffy, 2 to 3 minutes, scraping the side of the bowl. Slowly stream in the melted chocolate and mix until light and fluffy and thoroughly combined.

Assemble the cake by laying 1 layer on a serving platter. Top with ½ cup/118 ml of the buttercream, then with a third of the crunch. Repeat with the second layer, then top the cake with the third layer. Top the cake with the remaining buttercream and spread over the top and sides of the cake. Sprinkle with the remaining crunch.

BLACK TEA CAKE *with* BLACKBERRY LIME JAM *and* HONEY WHIPPED CREAM

This is one of those super versatile cakes that can easily take on almost any character. For an easy, casual brunch, just keep things simple and put the cake out with whipped cream and jam on the side. For a rustic yet composed dessert, assemble the cakes with pretty (but not perfect!) layers of all the components. And if I really want to get fancy, I'll top the cake with gold-painted fresh blackberries.

MAKES 8 TO 10 SERVINGS

For the blackberry jam

- 3½ cups (455 g) fresh or frozen blackberries
- 3 tablespoons freshly squeezed lime juice
- ½ cup (100 g) granulated sugar
- 1 tablespoon plus 1 teaspoon cornstarch

For the cake

- 2 tablespoons black tea leaves
- 2 cups (240 g) all-purpose flour
- 1 teaspoon baking powder
- ½ teaspoon baking soda
- ½ cup (125 ml) whole milk
- 2 tablespoons lime zest
- ½ cup (125 ml) freshly squeezed lime juice
- 1¾ cups (350 g) granulated sugar
- 3 large eggs, at room temperature
- 1 cup (250 ml) extra-virgin olive oil

For the honey whipped cream

- 4 teaspoons chilled water
- 1 teaspoon unflavored gelatin
- 1 cup (250 ml) heavy whipping cream
- ¼ cup (65 ml) honey

TO MAKE THE BLACKBERRY JAM: In a blender or food processor, blend together the blackberries, lime juice, sugar, and cornstarch until completely smooth. Transfer the purée to a medium saucepan. Cook over medium heat, stirring, until boiling. Remove from the heat and set aside to cool completely.

Preheat the oven to 350°F (180°C). Line two 8-inch/ 20.5 cm round baking pans with parchment paper and set aside.

TO MAKE THE CAKE: In a spice or coffee grinder, blend the tea leaves to a fine powder. In a large bowl, combine the tea, flour, baking powder, and baking soda. Set aside.

In a medium bowl, whisk together the milk and the lime zest and juice. Set aside.

In a large bowl, using an electric mixer on high speed, beat the sugar and eggs until light and fluffy, 3 to 5 minutes. Slowly pour the olive oil into the egg mixture, continuing to beat until emulsified, 3 to 5 minutes. Beating on low speed, starting and ending with the flour mixture, alternate adding the flour mixture and milk mixture in 3 additions.

Divide the batter equally between the prepared pans and bake until a toothpick inserted into the center comes out clean, 35 to 40 minutes. Remove from the oven and transfer the pans to a wire rack to cool completely.

(directions continue)

WHEN READY TO ASSEMBLE THE CAKE, MAKE THE HONEY WHIPPED CREAM: Place the chilled water in a shallow, microwave-safe bowl and sprinkle the gelatin evenly over the top. Let the mixture stand for about 5 minutes, or until the gelatin blooms and the mixture is solid.

Place the bowl in a microwave and heat on LOW for 10 seconds, or until the mixture reaches a syruplike consistency.

In a large bowl, using an electric mixer on medium speed, whip the cream until thick, 2 to 3 minutes. With the mixer on its lowest setting, add the honey and beat until combined, about 1 minute, then slowly add the gelatin mixture and mix until soft peaks form, 1 to 2 minutes.

Assemble the cake by placing 1 cake layer on a serving platter. Top with half of the blackberry jam and spread it evenly over the cake. Layer with half of the honey whipped cream and spread evenly. Repeat with the second cake layer and top with the remaining jam and most of the honey whipped cream. Finish with a very thin layer of the remaining honey whipped cream for a smooth and polished naked cake appearance.

RASPBERRY LEMONADE CUPCAKES

While I was growing up, my mom made a lot of lemonade, but never the fresh kind. It was always the powdery mix, though back then I never knew the difference. The first time I had it fresh, I thought it was too tart. So, as with most things, I tinkered around until I made it to my liking. Adding raspberries to the mix lent sweetness to the bright citrus and balanced the whole thing out. It's a combination I love so much that I've added it to my cupcake repertoire.

MAKES 12 SERVINGS

For the lemon cupcakes

- 1½ cups (180 g) all-purpose flour
- 1½ teaspoons baking powder
- ½ teaspoon salt
- ⅓ cup (80 ml) buttermilk
- ⅓ cup (80 ml) freshly squeezed lemon juice
- ½ cup (113 g) unsalted butter, at room temperature
- 1 cup (200 g) granulated sugar
- 2 teaspoons freshly grated lemon zest
- 2 large eggs

For the raspberry buttercream

- ½ cup (113 g) unsalted butter, at room temperature
- 1 (1.2 ounce/4 g) package freeze-dried raspberries, ground to a fine crumb
- 3 cups (360 g) confectioners' sugar
- ½ cup (120 ml) heavy whipping cream, plus more if needed
- ¼ teaspoon salt

For the topping

- 12 fresh raspberries
- Sprinkles

Directions

Preheat the oven to 350°F (180°C). Line one 12-cup muffin tin with foil or baking cups and set aside.

TO MAKE THE CUPCAKES: In a medium bowl, whisk together the flour, baking powder, and salt; set aside. In a large mixing cup, stir together the buttermilk and lemon juice; set aside.

In a large bowl, using an electric mixer on medium speed, cream together the butter, granulated sugar, and lemon zest until light and fluffy, 2 to 3 minutes. Add the eggs, 1 at a time, mixing well between each addition. Scrape down the sides of the bowl, and beating on low speed, starting and ending with the flour mixture, alternate adding the flour mixture and the buttermilk mixture, beating until just combined.

Divide the batter evenly among the prepared muffin cups, filling each cup about three-quarters full. Bake until golden on top and a toothpick inserted into the center of a cupcake comes out clean, 20 to 22 minutes.

Remove from the oven and allow the cupcakes to cool in the tin for 5 minutes before transferring them to a wire rack to cool completely.

WHEN READY TO ASSEMBLE THE CUPCAKES, MAKE THE BUTTERCREAM: In a large bowl, beat the butter with an electric mixer for about 1 minute, or until it's smooth and creamy, then add the ground raspberries and sift in the confectioners' sugar. Add the cream and salt and beat the buttercream until it's light and fluffy, 2 to 3 minutes. If the frosting is too thick, add 1 teaspoon of cream at a time to reach a smooth, creamy consistency.

Transfer the buttercream to a pastry bag fitted with a Wilton 1M tip and pipe the frosting on top of the cupcakes. Top each with a fresh raspberry and sprinkles.

SINGLE SERVINGS

What is it about miniature desserts that makes them so much more special? Maybe it's the idea of getting your very own little jar or bite, or maybe it's just because they're so darn cute. These pint-size gems are just as at home on your kitchen counter for snack time as they are at a polished dinner party.

LEMON MARSHMALLOW PIE POPS

Food on a stick never fails to draw me in, so naturally, sweets on a stick are a must in my baking and entertaining repertoire. I do all kinds of pies on sticks, but this lemon marshmallow version almost always gets the most attention. Rerolling pie dough can make for a tough crust, so I reroll the scraps and save them in the freezer to make decorative pie toppings in other recipes. Then, nothing goes to waste.

MAKES 8 TO 10 PIE POPS

2   recipes Pie Dough (page 100)

1   large egg, at room temperature

¾   cup (240 g) lemon curd

2   egg whites, at room temperature

1   cup (200 g) granulated sugar

½   teaspoon pure vanilla extract

¼   teaspoon salt

Directions

Preheat the oven to 350°F (180°C).

On a lightly floured surface, roll out each pie dough disk to ⅛-inch/3 mm thickness. Using a 2½-inch/6.5 cm biscuit cutter, stamp out a total of 16 to 20 circles, without rerolling the dough scraps (see headnote). Whisk the egg together with 1 tablespoon of water. Brush the borders of the dough rounds with egg wash. Lay one end of a wooden Popsicle stick flat over each dough round. Place 1 tablespoon of lemon curd in the center of each pie dough round, leaving a ¼-inch/6 mm border. Place a second dough round on top and crimp the edges with fork tines. Brush the top and bottom sides of the pie pop with remaining egg wash. Continue assembling pie pops from the remaining dough and lemon curd.

Bake for 10 to 12 minutes, or until the crust is golden brown. Remove the pie pops from the baking sheet and transfer to a wire rack to cool completely.

TO MAKE THE MARSHMALLOW CREME: In the meantime, make the marshmallow creme. Place the egg whites and sugar in a medium, heatproof bowl set over a pot of simmering water, making sure that the bottom of the bowl does not touch the water. Whisking constantly, cook until the temperature of the mixture reaches 165°F (71°C), 3 to 5 minutes. Remove the bowl from the heat and, using an electric mixer on high speed, beat until the marshmallow cream doubles in volume, forms stiff peaks, and cools to room temperature, 10 to 12 minutes. Beat in vanilla extract and salt. Dip the pie pops in the marshmallow cream, lay flat on the baking sheet, and, using a kitchen torch, lightly toast.

MINI CINNAMON ROLLS

I don't know how it happened, but my boys and their dad have some-how become cinnamon roll experts. And by experts, I mean they have turned up their nose at several of my cinnamon roll productions. I've tried sworn recipes from newspapers and magazines, but alas, no takers. Then I happened upon this pop-able version. It's ooey and gooey in all the right ways, and it never fails to lead to a licked-clean pan just minutes after being pulled from the oven.

MAKES 24 MINI CINNAMON ROLLS

For the dough

1 (¼ ounce/10 g) packet active dry yeast

3 tablespoons hot water (between 105° and 110°F)

3 tablespoons granulated sugar

1 large egg, at room temperature

½ teaspoon salt

¼ cup (55 g) unsalted butter, at room temperature

⅓ cup (80 ml) buttermilk

2½ cups (300 g) all purpose flour, plus more for dusting

Nonstick cooking spray

For the cinnamon filling

½ cup (100 g) light brown sugar

¼ cup (55 g) unsalted butter

2 teaspoons ground cinnamon

⅛ teaspoon salt

Nonstick cooking spray

(ingredients continue)

For the icing

2   cups (240 g) confectioners' sugar

¼   cup (55 g) unsalted butter, melted

¼   cup (60 ml) heavy whipping cream or half-and-half

½   teaspoon vanilla bean paste

⅛   teaspoon salt

Directions ....

TO MAKE THE DOUGH: In a small dish, sprinkle the yeast over the hot water and set aside for 10 minutes until the yeast activates and bubbles appear.

Meanwhile, mix together the granulated sugar, egg, and salt in a large bowl. Place the butter in a medium saucepan over low heat and cook, stirring, until melted. Turn off the heat and stir in the buttermilk. Add the buttermilk mixture to the egg mixture; stir to combine.

Add the yeast mixture to the bowl; stir to combine. Add the flour and stir with a wooden spoon just until it all starts to come together. Then, hand knead until the dough starts to come together into a ball and becomes soft and smooth, 2 to 3 minutes. Remove the dough from the bowl and lightly coat the inside of the bowl with nonstick cooking spray. Place the dough back in the bowl and cover it with plastic wrap. Set aside in a warm, draft-free place to rise and double in size, 1 to 1½ hours.

ONCE THE DOUGH HAS JUST ABOUT DOUBLED IN SIZE, MAKE THE CINNAMON FILLING: In a bowl, stir together the brown sugar, butter, cinnamon, and salt. Lightly coat the cups of a 24-cup mini muffin tin with nonstick cooking spray and set aside.

Divide the risen dough in half. Roll out half of the dough to a 5 x 12-inch/13 x 30 cm rectangle. Spread half of the cinnamon filling on top, leaving a ½-inch/1.3 cm border on one long side of rectangle. Starting with the filling-covered side, tightly roll the dough toward the opposite side.

Cut the log into 1-inch/2.5 cm pieces so you end up with 12 rolls, and place the cut pieces into the prepared tin, swirly side up. Repeat the process with remaining half of the dough and the cinnamon filling. Cover the pan and let the rolls rise until they are nearly doubled in size, about 30 minutes.

Meanwhile, preheat the oven to 350°F (180°C). When the rolls have risen, bake for 12 to 15 minutes, or until golden brown. Remove from the oven and set aside to cool slightly while you make the icing.

TO MAKE THE ICING: In a bowl, whisk all the icing ingredients together until the mixture is smooth. Carefully remove the cinnamon rolls from the pan and place on a serving tray. Drizzle the icing on top. Serve warm.

BUTTERSCOTCH CHOCOLATE CROISSANT BREAD PUDDINGS

This bread pudding is one of my favorite recipes to make for brunch—the individual serving method makes them extra-special. The end result is an elegant comfort dish that may quickly become a new staple.

MAKES 6 SERVINGS

8 to 10 chocolate croissants (1 pound/453 g in total), cut into 1-inch/2.5 cm cubes

1¼ cups (270 g) light brown sugar

½ cup (120 ml) heavy whipping cream

2 tablespoons unsalted butter

5 large eggs, at room temperature

1½ cups (380 ml) milk

1 teaspoon pure vanilla extract

½ teaspoon salt

½ cup (90 g) chopped semisweet or bittersweet chocolate

Confectioners' sugar, for dusting

Directions

Place the cut croissant pieces on a parchment-lined baking sheet and set aside to dry out while the custard portion is made.

In a medium saucepan, combine the brown sugar, cream, and butter. Bring to a boil and cook for 3 minutes. Remove from the heat and set aside to cool.

Preheat the oven to 350°F (180°C). Lightly butter six 6-ounce/177 ml small baking pots or ramekins and set them on a rimmed baking sheet.

In a large bowl, whisk together the eggs, milk, vanilla, and salt. Add the cooled brown sugar mixture and whisk just until combined. Carefully mix in the croissant pieces and chocolate. Evenly distribute the mixture among the pots.

Bake for 30 to 35 minutes, or until golden brown and puffed up. Let cool for 15 minutes before dusting with confectioners' sugar and serving warm.

RASPBERRY and PISTACHIO FRANGIPANE TARTS

If a tart and tea cakes had little tartlet babies, it would be this dessert. To punch things up in this recipe I added freeze dried raspberries over fresh ones for a more concentrated flavor. Along with that I gave, the traditional almond-based frangipane an update by using my favorite nuts pistachios. The tarts can be eaten cold or warm. I prefer it warm with a generous scoop of ice cream to go on top!

MAKES 6 (5-INCH/12.5 CM) TARTLETS

¾ cup (101 g) shelled unsalted pistachios, lightly toasted

⅓ cup (71 g) firmly packed light brown sugar

¼ teaspoon salt

1 large egg, lightly beaten

½ teaspoon pure vanilla extract

½ teaspoon almond extract

1 tablespoon unsalted butter, melted

1.2 ounces (34 g) freeze dried raspberries

Confectioners' sugar, for dusting

Directions

Preheat the oven to 375°F (190°C). Lightly cover six 5-inch/12.5 cm tartlet pans with nonstick spray.

Set aside two tablespoons (9 g) of pistachios. Place remaining ¾ cup (101 g) in a food processor and add the brown sugar, and salt. Process until mixture becomes finely ground. Add the egg, vanilla and almond extracts, and melted butter and process until the mixture comes together. Gently fold in half (0.6 oz. / 17 g) of the freeze dried raspberries, being careful not to overmix.

Pour the filling into the prepared tartlet pans halfway full. Bake until the frangipane is firm and golden brown, about 25 minutes.

Remove from the oven, transfer the tartlets to a wire rack, and allow to cool completely. Immediately before serving, chop remaining 2 tablespoons of pistachio to a coarse crumb and sprinkle on top of tartlets along with remaining (0.6 oz / 17 g) freeze dried raspberries. Dust with confectioners' sugar.

HONEY GRILLED PEACHES
with WHIPPED RICOTTA

Okay, so maybe it's not technically a tart or pie, but in spirit this dessert most certainly is. It took me a long time to come around to fruit-centric desserts, partly because the fruit was usually canned and swimming in slimy syrup. But when you take fresh late-summer peaches, give them a quick smoky char on the grill, and top them with a dollop of just-sweet-enough whipped ricotta, fruit gets taken to a whole new level.

MAKES 4 TO 6 SERVINGS

For the whipped ricotta

- 1 cup (240 g) ricotta cheese
- 4 ounces (110 g) cream cheese, at room temperature
- 3 tablespoons honey
- 3 tablespoons granulated sugar
- 1 teaspoon vanilla bean paste

For the grilled peaches

- Neutral oil, such as canola or grapeseed, as needed
- ¼ cup (60 ml) honey
- 1 tablespoon hot water
- 3 large ripe but firm peaches, halved and pitted

TO MAKE THE WHIPPED RICOTTA: Place the ricotta cheese, cream cheese, honey, sugar, and vanilla bean paste in a food processor. Pulse a few times until everything is combined and the mixture is light and fluffy in texture. Set aside.

TO MAKE THE GRILLED PEACHES: Heat a large grill pan over medium heat and brush with neutral oil. Whisk the honey with the hot water and brush it onto the cut side of the peaches. Grill the peaches, cut side down, until grill marks appear and the honey starts to caramelize, 3 to 5 minutes. Serve the grilled peaches with the whipped ricotta.

MOSCATO POACHED PLUMS over VANILLA WHIPPED CREAM

There's something magical that happens to fruit (especially plums) when its simmered in a Jacuzzi of sweet wine until plump, sweet, and all but falling apart at the touch of a spoon. It's like having the most decadent cake, no fussy baking required. I like serving wine-poached fruit over whipped cream, which rounds out the fruit's sweetness with its luscious, creamy richness.

MAKES 4 TO 6 SERVINGS

1   (750 ml) bottle Moscato or other sweet dessert wine

1   cup (213 g) packed light brown sugar

8   firm but ripe plums (about 2 pounds/907 g), cut in half and pitted

1   cup (250 ml) heavy whipping cream

3   tablespoons confectioners' sugar

2   teaspoons pure vanilla extract

Directions

In a large pot, combine the Moscato, 1 cup/240 ml of water, and the brown sugar and bring to a simmer, stirring occasionally. Add the plums and cook over medium heat for 5 to 10 minutes, or until the plums are tender but not overcooked.

Remove the plums from the poaching liquid and set aside to cool slightly.

In a large bowl, using an electric mixer on medium-high speed, beat together the cream, confectioners' sugar, and vanilla extract until soft peaks form.

Serve the plums warm with a dollop of whipped cream and a drizzle of the poaching liquid.

BLACK and WHITE PANNA COTTA

Silky, custardlike panna cotta is the little black dress of desserts—it easily suits any occasion with just the right accessories. This version perfectly suits a casual dinner with its confetti of chocolate shavings, but if you want, you could easily add wine-soaked fruits or even a little dusting of gold leaf for a little extra somethin' somethin'. And the best part? You can serve it in cute little individual jars (I love the ones Weck makes), which always has me reaching for my spoon.

MAKES 6 TO 8 (6-OUNCE/170 G) INDIVIDUAL-SIZE DESSERTS

2 cups (500 ml) heavy cream, separated

1 tablespoon gelatin

4 ounces (110 g) bittersweet chocolate, chopped finely

1 cup (250 ml) whole milk, separated

4 ounces (110 g) white chocolate, chopped finely

Chocolate shavings, for garnish

Raspberries, for garnish

Directions

TO MAKE THE BITTERSWEET CHOCOLATE LAYER: Sprinkle 1½ teaspoons of gelatin over 1 cup (250 ml) of the heavy cream in a medium sized saucepan. Set pan aside for 5 minutes to let gelatin bloom. Transfer pan over medium-low heat, cook and stir until mixture becomes warm and gelatin dissolves (make sure mixture does not come to a boil). Remove from heat and add the bittersweet chocolate, let sit for about 30 seconds for chocolate to melt slightly, then whisk until the mixture comes together and the chocolate is fully combined. Stir in ½ cup (120 ml) of the whole milk and evenly divide the mixture between 6 flutes.

Place the panna cotta in the refrigerator to set for about 1 hour, or until it is firm enough to layer with the white chocolate portion.

TO MAKE THE WHITE CHOCOLATE LAYER, follow the same instructions as the bittersweet layer while replacing the bittersweet chocolate addition with the white chocolate. Evenly divide and layer the white chocolate mixture on top of the bittersweet chocolate.

Return panna cotta to the refrigerator for at least 4 hours for both layers to fully set before serving.

Serve the panna cotta topped with chocolate shavings and raspberries.

STRAWBERRY and CREAM LAMINGTONS

Lamingtons are a traditional Australian cake that I was introduced to just a few years ago. I instantly fell in love with its pop-able bite-size cuteness. I've adapted the traditional sponge cake for one that is slightly denser. The buttercream is naturally stained from the strawberries. For a more intense hue, add a drop or two of soft pink gel food coloring.

MAKES 24 SQUARES

- 4 cups (480 g) all-purpose flour
- 2 teaspoons baking powder
- 1½ teaspoons baking soda
- 1½ teaspoons salt
- 1½ cups (375 ml) buttermilk
- ½ cup (120 ml) vegetable oil
- 2 teaspoons pure vanilla extract
- 2 teaspoons coconut extract
- 1 cup (225 g) unsalted butter, at room temperature
- 2 cups (400 g) granulated sugar

- 4 large eggs, at room temperature
- 1¼ ounce (34 g) freeze-dried strawberries
- 2½ cups (12.5 ounces/417 g) strawberries, hulled and sliced
- 8 cups (908 g) confectioners' sugar, divided
- ¾ cup (170 g) unsalted butter, at room temperature
- 2 teaspoons pure vanilla extract
- ¼ teaspoon salt
- 1 pound (453 g) sweetened shredded coconut flakes

Directions

Preheat the oven to 350°F (180°C). Line two 13 x 9-inch/ 33 x 23 cm baking pans with parchment paper.

In a large bowl, combine the flour, baking powder, baking soda, and salt. Set aside.

In a medium bowl, whisk together the buttermilk, vegetable oil, and vanilla and coconut extracts. Set aside.

In a large bowl, using an electric mixer on medium speed, cream together the butter and granulated sugar until light and fluffy, 3 to 5 minutes. Beat in the eggs, 1 at a time. Scrape the bottom and sides of the bowl. Beating at low speed, starting and ending with the flour mixture, alternate adding the flour mixture and buttermilk mixture in 3 additions. Divide the mixture equally among the prepared pans and bake for 35 to 40 minutes, or until a toothpick inserted into the center comes out clean. Remove from the oven and transfer the pans to a wire rack to cool completely.

In a blender process the freeze-dried strawberries to a fine crumb. Add the fresh strawberries and process until smooth. Press the strawberry mixture through a fine-mesh sieve into a small saucepot. Bring to a boil over medium-high heat and cook, stirring occasionally, until reduced by half. Remove from the heat and allow to cool completely.

When ready to assemble the cake, make the butter-cream: In a bowl, combine 6 cups/680 g of the confectioners' sugar and the butter, vanilla, salt, and cooled strawberry mixture. Using an electric mixer on medium speed, beat until light and fluffy. If the frosting is too wet, add the remaining 2 cups/228 g of confectioners' sugar, ½ cup/60 g at a time, until it reaches the desired consistency.

Assemble the cake by placing 1 cake layer on a cutting board. Spread with 2 cups/475 ml of the buttercream. Place the remaining cake layer on top and, using a serrated knife, cut the cake into two dozen 2-inch/5 cm squares. Spread the remaining buttercream over the tops and sides of the cake squares, then sprinkle with coconut on all sides.

BANANAS FOSTER PUDDING PARFAITS

This is one of those classic desserts to which I gave a modern update by replacing the pyrotechnics with a simple pan sauté. And then I flipped it into a pudding parfait and finished with brûléed bananas and a sprinkling of caramel popcorn for a crunchy fun finish.

MAKES 6 (8-OUNCE/235 ML) SERVINGS

For the pudding

1   cup (200 g) granulated sugar

2½ cups (590 ml) whole milk, divided

4   tablespoons cornstarch

3   large eggs

2   tablespoons gold rum

2   teaspoons pure vanilla extract

1   teaspoon kosher salt

For the whipped cream topping

1   cup (240 ml) heavy whipping cream

¼   cup (50 g) granulated sugar

For the brûléed bananas

3   medium bananas, peeled and cut on a diagonal into ¼-inch/6 mm slices

¼   cup (60 g) demerara sugar

1   ounce (31 g) caramel corn

Directions

TO MAKE THE PUDDING: In a medium saucepan over medium-high heat, bring the granulated sugar and ¼ cup/60 ml of water to a boil, using the handle of the pan to swirl the mixture (do not stir directly). Cook until a dark amber color is reached, about 7 minutes. Remove the pan from the heat and carefully add 1½ cups/350 ml of the milk, as the mixture will bubble wildly.

In a large liquid measuring cup, whisk together remaining 1 cup/240 ml of milk and the cornstarch. Add the eggs and whisk until combined. Add the milk mixture to the caramelized sugar mixture. Return the pan to medium-high heat and cook until thickened, making sure to stir continuously, 5 to 7 minutes. Remove from the heat and stir in the rum, vanilla, and salt. Set aside for 15 minutes to cool slightly. Place plastic wrap directly on the surface and transfer to the refrigerator to chill completely, about 4 hours.

TO MAKE THE WHIPPED CREAM TOPPING: In a large bowl, using an electric mixer on medium-high speed, whip the cream and granulated sugar until soft peaks form. Set aside.

TO MAKE THE BRÛLÉED BANANAS: Sprinkle the cut side of the banana slices with demerara sugar, then use a kitchen torch to brûlée until browned and toasted.

Assemble the parfaits by evenly dividing the pudding and whipped cream among six 8-ounce/235 ml cups. Top with the banana slices and caramel corn.

MINI CHOCOLATE BANOFFEE PIES

I flipped the traditional banoffee pie to the chocolate version you see here to temper the sweetness of the classic dulce de leche profile.

MAKES 6 (4-INCH/10 CM) OR 5 (5-INCH/12.5 CM) MINI PIES

- 3 cups (210 g) whole chocolate wafer cookies
- ½ cup (113 g) cold unsalted butter
- 4 ounces (115 g) bittersweet chocolate, chopped
- 2 cups (480 ml) store-bought dulce de leche
- ¼ teaspoon salt
- 1½ cups (370 ml) heavy whipping cream
- 2 tablespoons confectioners' sugar
- 3 bananas (about 1 pound/453 g), sliced ¼ inch/6 mm thick
- Chocolate sauce, for drizzling

Directions

Preheat the oven to 350°F (180°C). Have ready six 4-inch/10 cm or five 5 inch/12.5 cm mini pie pans.

In a food processor, pulse the chocolate wafers until a fine crumb forms. Add the butter and pulse for 30 seconds, or until the mixture is the texture of wet sand.

Divide the mixture among the mini pie pans and press into the pan to form a crust.

Place the mini pie pans on a baking sheet. Bake for 5 to 7 minutes, or until the crust is dry on the edges and starting to brown. Remove from the oven and allow to cool completely.

In a double boiler, melt the chocolate. Add the dulce de leche and salt and gently fold to combine.

Divide the chocolate dulce de leche equally among the chocolate crusts and chill for at least 1 hour.

In a large bowl, using an electric mixer on medium-high speed, beat together the cream and confectioners' sugar until soft peaks form.

Assemble the pies by topping each mini pie with about ½ cup/75 g of banana slices, a dollop of whipped cream, and a drizzle of chocolate sauce. Serve immediately.

RASPBERRY ÉCLAIRS with VANILLA BEAN CREAM

These elegant bite-size treats look much harder to make than they really are. But no one needs to know that but you. Make this for your next party, and your guests will be clamoring for more of these éclairs.

MAKES ABOUT 28 ÉCLAIRS

For the dough

- ½ cup (120 ml) whole milk
- 6 tablespoons (84 g) unsalted butter
- 1 tablespoon granulated sugar
- 1¼ teaspoons kosher salt
- 1 cup (120 g) bread flour
- 3 large eggs

For the vanilla pastry cream

- 3 cups (750 ml) whole milk
- 1 vanilla bean, split lengthwise
- ⅔ cup (226 g) granulated sugar
- ¼ cup (30 g) cornstarch
- ½ teaspoon salt
- 4 large egg yolks, at room temperature
- 2 tablespoons unsalted butter, at room temperature

For the raspberry glaze

- 2 cups (240 g) confectioners' sugar
- 5 tablespoons raspberry purée
- 1 drop of pink food coloring

- 2 ounces (55 g) dark chocolate, melted (optional)

  Edible gold leaf (optional)

  Fresh raspberries, sliced

188

Directions ....

Line 2 baking sheets with parchment paper. Fit a pastry bag with a ½-inch/1.3 cm star tip (the shells will crack less with a star tip versus a round tip).

TO MAKE THE DOUGH: Combine the milk, ½ cup/120 ml of water, and the butter, granulated sugar, and salt in a medium saucepan over medium heat. Once the butter is melted, bring the mixture to a simmer. Then, remove the pan from the heat and add the flour all at once. Using a sturdy spatula or wooden spoon, stir until streaks of flour are no longer visible. Return the pan to medium heat and vigorously stir the dough, smashing it against the side of the pan. The idea is to cook the moisture out of the dough. The dough is ready when it starts to pull away from the side and a visible film is on the bottom of the pan, 3 to 5 minutes.

Transfer the mixture to a large bowl, and using an electric mixer, beat on low speed for 3 minutes to release the steam. Let stand for 10 minutes to cool.

Preheat the oven to 350°F (180°C). In a small bowl, beat the eggs until blended.

With the mixer on medium speed, beat half of the egg mixture into the dough, making sure the eggs are well incorporated into the dough before adding the remaining egg mixture. The dough is ready when it's smooth, glossy, and a tip forms when the beaters are dipped in and pulled out of the dough, and immediately falls in on itself.

Transfer the dough to a pastry bag. Pipe 4-inch/10 cm-long shells onto the prepared baking sheets, making sure to space each shell 2 inches apart. Bake for 20 minutes, turning the pan halfway through. Remove the shells from the oven, and working quickly, cut a ⅛ inch/1.3 cm long slit in the top of each éclair.

TO MAKE THE VANILLA PASTRY CREAM: In a medium saucepan over medium-high heat, combine the milk and vanilla bean and seeds. Bring the mixture to a simmer, then remove from the heat. Cover with plastic wrap and let the vanilla steep in the milk for 20 to 30 minutes. Remove the vanilla bean.

In a medium saucepan, whisk together the sugar, cornstarch, salt, and egg yolks. Add the milk mixture and whisk to completely combine. Bring to a boil over medium-high heat, whisking constantly, until very thick. Remove from the heat and pour the mixture through a sieve into a large bowl. Stir in the butter. Cover the surface of the pastry cream with plastic wrap and let cool completely in the refrigerator, about 2 hours.

TO MAKE RASPBERRY GLAZE: Combine all the glaze ingredients and whisk until well blended.

To assemble the éclairs, fit a pastry bag with a small, round tip and fill with the vanilla pastry cream. Pipe the inside of each éclair with about 2 tablespoons of the pastry cream. Dip the top of each éclair into the glaze. Optional: Pipe chocolate stripes on top, place a piece of gold leaf on each, and press a sliced raspberry, cut side up, on top.

CINNAMON and SUGAR FUNNEL CAKE BITES

Admittedly, I didn't try funnel cake until I was in my twenties, but it was an instant love affair. What's not to love about dough that's deep-fried and dusted with confectioners' sugar? This churrolike cinnamon and sugar version is my twist on the amusement park classic, and is now a must-make recipe for my little guy, who loves the way these crispy bites are perfectly palm-size.

MAKES 30 TO 40 CAKE BITES

Vegetable or canola oil, for deep-frying (about 2 quarts/1.9 L)

2 teaspoons ground cinnamon

¾ cup (150 g) granulated sugar, divided

2 large eggs

1 cup (250 ml) milk

1 teaspoon pure vanilla extract

3 cups (360 g) all-purpose flour

1 tablespoon baking powder

¼ teaspoon salt

Directions

Pour oil to a depth of at least 3 inches/7.5 cm into a large, heavy saucepan and heat over high heat to 350°F (180°C) on a deep-frying thermometer, adjusting the heat as you go, to maintain the oil temperature.

In a medium shallow dish, combine the cinnamon and ½ cup/100 g of the sugar. Set aside.

In a large bowl, combine the eggs, milk, 1 cup/236.5 ml of water, and the vanilla.

In a medium bowl, combine the flour, the remaining ¼ cup/50 g of sugar, and the baking powder and salt. Add the flour mixture to the egg mixture and whisk well to combine, making sure no flour lumps remain. Ladle the mixture into a squeeze bottle or funnel.

Carefully squeeze about ¼ cup/60 ml of the batter into the hot oil while moving the bottle in a circular motion to create spiral-like shapes. Fry the funnel cakes for 2 to 3 minutes, or until golden brown and slightly puffed. Using a stainless-steel skimmer or tongs, remove the funnel cakes from the oil and transfer them to a paper towel–lined plate to drain for 1 minute.

Toss the warm funnel cakes in the cinnamon-sugar mixture. Repeat with the remaining batter, allowing the oil to come back to the right temperature between batches.

Serve warm.

HOT CHOCOLATE *and* ROASTED MARSHMALLOW POTS *de* CRÈME

*This dessert perfectly marries childhood nostalgia with adult sophistication. It has all the trappings of those pudding cups many of us unpacked from our lunches at school, but with a name like **pots de crème** (French for "pudding")—and eggs in the base instead of cornstarch, which give the pudding a much silkier texture and truer chocolate flavor—it's tempting to eat this with your pinkie up. To keep it from getting too fancy-shmancy, though, I love serving this dessert in individual coffee mugs and topping each with toasted marshmallows, hot chocolate style.*

MAKES 8 SERVINGS

For the pots de crème

- 1½ cups (255 g) chopped dark chocolate (60–70% cacao)
- 2 cups (500 ml) heavy whipping cream
- 1 cup (250 ml) milk
- 2 tablespoons unsweetened cocoa powder
- ½ teaspoon kosher salt
- 6 large egg yolks, at room temperature
- ¼ cup (50 g) granulated sugar
- 1 teaspoon pure vanilla extract

For the marshmallows

- Nonstick cooking spray
- 3 tablespoons unflavored gelatin powder
- 2 cups (400 g) granulated sugar
- ¼ cup (65 ml) honey
- ½ teaspoon vanilla bean paste
- ⅔ cup (59 g) confectioners' sugar
- 3 tablespoons cornstarch

Directions

TO MAKE THE POTS DE CRÈME: Preheat the oven to 300°F (150°C). Set eight 4-ounce/115 ml heatproof espresso cups or 4-ounce/115 ml ramekins in a roasting pan.

Place the chopped chocolate in a large bowl. Set aside.

In a large saucepan, over medium heat, stir together the cream, milk, cocoa powder, and salt, and bring to a simmer. Remove from the heat.

In a second large bowl, whisk together the egg yolks, granulated sugar, and vanilla. Whisking constantly, slowly pour the hot cream mixture into the yolk mixture. Whisk until fully combined and smooth. Strain through a fine-mesh sieve into the bowl of chocolate. Let stand for 2 minutes, then whisk until well combined and smooth. Transfer the custard to a large pitcher for easy pouring.

Divide the custard among the prepared espresso cups. Set the pan in the oven, and carefully pour hot water into the pan to come halfway up the sides of the espresso cups.

Bake the custards for 30 to 35 minutes, or until set around the edges but the center jiggles when the side of the cup is tapped. Carefully remove from the oven and transfer the cups to a wire rack to cool completely. Chill in the refrigerator for at least 4 hours.

TO MAKE THE MARSHMALLOWS: Lightly coat a 9-inch/23 cm square baking pan with nonstick cooking spray. Place parchment paper on top, leaving a 1-inch/2.5 cm overhang on 2 opposite sides. Then coat the paper with nonstick cooking spray. (The first layer of nonstick spray will help keep the parchment paper in place.)

Place ¼ cup/59 ml of water in a large bowl and sprinkle the gelatin over the surface. Leave untouched to bloom.

In a medium saucepan over medium heat, make a syrup by combining the granulated sugar, honey, and ¼ cup/59 ml of water; stirring only until the sugar dissolves. Bring the mixture to a simmer and cook, without stirring, until a candy thermometer reads 240°F (116°C), 12 to 15 minutes.

Beating with an electric mixer on low, pour the sugar mixture into the gelatin mixture in a steady stream. Beat on low speed until combined, then increase the speed to high and beat until the mixture is thick and fluffy and tripled in volume, about 10 minutes. Add the vanilla bean paste and beat until combined, about 1 minute.

Using a lightly oiled spatula, scrape the mixture into the prepared baking pan. Smooth out the top (the top surface will not be completely even). Set aside in a cool place (not the refrigerator) for 8 hours or overnight.

In a bowl, whisk together the confectioners' sugar and cornstarch. Remove the marshmallow from the pan and peel away the parchment paper. Using a sieve, lightly dust the top and bottom of the marshmallow with the confectioners' sugar mixture. Lightly coat a serrated knife with nonstick cooking spray and slice the marshmallow into 1-inch/2.5 cm cubes. Cover the cut sides with the confectioners' sugar mixture. The marshmallows will keep in an airtight container between layers of nonstick parchment for 3 to 4 days.

Set the marshmallows on a baking sheet. Toast the marshmallows with a kitchen torch. Let the toasted marshmallows rest for a minute, until slightly cooled, then divide the toasted marshmallow cubes among the tops of the pots de crème.

CONFECTIONS

There are few things sweeter than receiving a box of chocolates, but there's almost nothing more special than receiving one that is filled with homemade confections. They are surprisingly easier to make than most people think. The key is having all the ingredients and tools ready to go at the start of the recipe.

MOCHA CRUNCH FUDGE

This is a favorite around the holidays. I like to make it and give it as gifts because it's easy to make and everyone loves the creamy richness of the fudge contrasted against the crunch bottom.

MAKES 40 TO 50 (1-INCH/2.5 CM) SQUARES

Nonstick cooking spray

1½ cups (300 g) granulated sugar

¾ cup (190 ml) half-and-half

¼ cup (55 g) unsalted butter

½ teaspoon salt

1½ teaspoons instant espresso powder

3 cups (135 g) mini marshmallows

12 ounces (340 g) semisweet chocolate chips

1 teaspoon pure vanilla extract

1½ cups (170 g) Whopper candies, roughly chopped

Directions

Line an 8-inch/20.5 cm baking pan with parchment paper and spray with non-stick cooking spray.

In a medium saucepan, combine the sugar, half-and-half, butter, salt, and espresso powder. Bring to a boil and cook for 5 minutes over medium heat. Turn off the heat and add the marsh-mallows and chocolate, quickly stirring the mixture until everything is melted and combined. Stir in the vanilla. Pour just enough of the mixture to cover the bottom of the prepared pan. Sprinkle the chopped malt balls evenly on top. Pour the remaining mixture evenly on top. Let cool at room temperature for 30 minutes before transferring to the refrigerator to set for at least 4 hours. Cut the fudge into 1-inch/2.5 cm squares. Store the fudge in a tightly covered container in the refrigerator. Bring to room temperature before serving.

FRUIT and NUT MATZO BRITTLE

Admittedly, I'm a big fan of barks, brittles, and candies because they require so little work while delivering big on flavor and presentation. They're also the perfect vehicle for a pantry clean-out, especially when you find yourself with an overabundance of dried fruit and nuts.

MAKES ABOUT 30 PIECES OF CANDY

4 to 6 sheets unsalted matzos

1 cup (225 g) unsalted butter, cut into chunks

1 cup (215 g) firmly packed light brown sugar

2 teaspoons flaky sea salt

½ teaspoon pure vanilla extract

1 cup (175 g) bittersweet chocolate chips

2 ounces (55 g) white chocolate, melted

⅔ cup (112 g) salted and shelled pistachios, chopped

3 tablespoons finely chopped candied ginger

3 tablespoons finely chopped dried mango

Preheat the oven to 375°F (190°C). Line a 17 x 11-inch/ 43 x 28 cm baking sheet with foil, making sure the foil goes up and over the edges by 1 inch/2.5 cm. Cover the foil with a sheet of parchment paper. Cover the bottom of the pan with the matzo crackers, breaking up pieces as needed to cover the surface completely.

In a medium saucepan over medium-high heat, cook the butter and brown sugar, stirring, until the mixture begins to boil. Once boiling, stir once, then lower the heat and simmer; holding the handle of the pot, swirl occasionally, until the mixture is golden brown and syrupy, 8 to 10 minutes.

Remove from the heat, add the salt and vanilla, and immediately pour and spread the mixture over the matzo.

Bake for 7 to 10 minutes, watching to make sure it doesn't burn. If it appears to be burning, lower the heat to 350°F (180°C).

Remove from the oven and transfer to a wire rack. Immediately cover with the bittersweet chocolate chips. Let stand for 5 minutes, then spread the melted bitter-sweet chocolate with an offset spatula. Drizzle with the melted white chocolate. Sprinkle with the candied ginger, dried mango, and pistachios. Let cool on the baking sheet, 30 to 45 minutes, before breaking into pieces.

SALTED CHOCOLATE and CARAMEL CASHEW CLUSTERS

When I was younger, my sister and I would make candy runs to the convenience store around the corner from where we lived. We would beg, hustle, and scrape up loose change from around the house so as to score a bag filled half with candy, half with empty wrappers (from all the candy we ate on the walk home). Nowadays, I scratch the candy itch by making these caramels.

MAKES ABOUT 4 DOZEN CLUSTERS

Nonstick cooking spray

1½ cups (300 g) granulated sugar

¼ cup (60 ml) Lyle's golden syrup or light corn syrup

1 cup (250 ml) heavy whipping cream

6 tablespoons (85 g) unsalted butter

2 teaspoons flaky sea salt, plus more for sprinkling

1 pound (455 g) unsalted whole raw cashews

12 ounces (340 g) bittersweet chocolate (60% cacao or more)

Directions

Line an 8-inch/20.5 cm square baking pan with parchment paper, leaving a 3-inch/7.5 cm overhang on 2 opposite sides. Lightly coat the parchment with nonstick cooking spray.

In a large saucepan, combine the sugar and syrup with ¼ cup/60 ml of water. Bring to a boil over medium heat and cook until golden brown, 7 to 9 minutes. Don't stir the mixture as it cooks; rather, holding the handle of the pot, gently swirl the mixture around the pan.

Lower the heat to medium-low and carefully add the cream, butter, and salt. The mixture will bubble violently. Continue to cook for 7 to 9 minutes, or until a candy thermometer reads 250°F (121°C). Remove the caramel from the heat and stir in the cashews. Pour the mixture into the prepared pan and let it harden in the refrigerator for at least 1 to 2 hours.

Using the overhanging parchment paper as makeshift handles, lift the caramel out of the pan and place on a cutting board. Lightly coat the blade of a knife with nonstick cooking spray and cut the caramel into 3 x ½-inch/7.5 x 1.3 cm pieces. Set aside.

To make the chocolate coating, place the chocolate in a heatproof bowl over a pot of barely simmering water, making sure the bottom of the bowl is not touching the water. Stir occasionally, until the chocolate is melted. Remove from the heat. Alternatively, in a microwave-safe bowl, melt the chocolate in a microwave on MEDIUM-HIGH in 10 second bursts, stirring between each burst (or melt in a double boiler).

Drizzle 1 tablespoon of chocolate over each caramel and sprinkle with flaky sea salt. Allow the chocolate to cool and harden, at least 2 to 3 hours.

Wrap each piece in parchment and store in the refrigerator. Bring the candies back to room temperature before serving.

BEER and PRETZEL TRUFFLES

When I first started baking, I would really try to push the limits and combine, fuse, and mash up pretty much any flavors or ingredients that appealed to me. Some were hits, some were misses, some were memorable—some were just downright embarrassing. But this sweet-savory treat was one of my earliest discoveries that I love just as much now as I did then. Their novelty is just as fun as their rich, deep flavor, which makes them perfect for parties or for giving as gifts.

MAKES 14 TO 16 DOZEN TRUFFLES

8 ounces (227 g) bittersweet chocolate, finely chopped

1 cup (250 ml) stout beer

2 ounces (55 g) pretzels

Directions

Place the chopped chocolate in a large, shallow, heatproof bowl. Set aside.

In a small saucepan over medium heat, cook the beer, stirring, until the liquid is reduced by half, 5 to 7 minutes. Pour the hot beer reduction over the chocolate. Set aside for 2 minutes, then gently stir until the chocolate is smooth and fully melted. Allow to cool to room temperature.

Cover and refrigerate the chocolate mixture until set, 2 to 3 hours.

In a food processor, blend the pretzels to a coarse crumb. Alternatively, place the pretzels in a resealable plastic bag and use a rolling pin to crush them. Transfer the crumbs to a small bowl and set aside.

Line a 13 x 9-inch/33 x 23 cm baking pan with parchment paper and set aside.

Use a melon baller, scoop out 1½-inch/4 cm balls. Transfer to the prepared pan. Continue until all the balls are formed. Set aside to warm slightly. Roll each truffle in crushed pretzels. If the truffles become too soft to work with, transfer the pan to the refrigerator to chill slightly.

Keep the truffles refrigerated until ready to serve. Let stand at room temperature for 20 minutes prior to serving.

RAINBOW RIPPLED MERINGUE KISSES

If ever there were a happier cookie, I haven't met it. These colorful, pinwheel-like meringues never fail to make me smile when I pull them out of the oven—it's like a celebration of happiness! They're also a great canvas for adding different flavors of extracts, such as peppermint or orange. Just add a teaspoon of your preferred flavor instead of vanilla.

MAKES ABOUT 5 DOZEN MERINGUE KISSES

4   large egg whites

¼   teaspoon cream of tartar

1   cup (200 g) granulated sugar

1   teaspoon pure vanilla extract

Red food coloring (preferably gel food coloring)

Directions

Preheat the oven to 250°F (120°C). Line 2 baking sheets with parchment paper and fit a pastry bag with a small star tip.

In a large bowl, using an electric mixer on low speed, whisk the egg whites and cream of tartar until small bubbles start to form around the edge of the egg whites. Increase the speed to high and whip until soft peaks form, 1 to 2 minutes. Slowly add the sugar, ¼ cup/50 g at a time, and continue to beat on high speed until the mixture is stiff and glossy, 3 to 4 minutes. Whisk in the vanilla.

Using a small paintbrush, paint 2 or 3 stripes of red food coloring inside the prepared pastry bag. Fill the pastry bag with meringue. Pipe 1½-inch/4 cm star shapes onto prepared baking sheets, about 1 inch/2.5 cm apart, 30 to a sheet. Refill the pastry bag as necessary, adding more food coloring as needed.

Bake the meringues for about 1 hour, or until firm to the touch. Turn off the oven, propping open its door with a wooden spoon handle, and leave the meringues to cool for a couple of hours or overnight.

APPLE PIE MARSHMALLOWS

For the marshmallows

Nonstick cooking spray

¼ cup (58 ml) unfiltered apple juice

3 tablespoons gelatin

2 cups (400 g) granulated sugar

½ cup (120 g) water

¼ cup (65 ml) honey

1 (1.2-ounce/34 g) package freeze-dried apples, pulverized to a crumb, divided

For the topping

5 tablespoons all-purpose flour

3 tablespoons light brown sugar

1 tablespoon granulated sugar

¾ teaspoon ground cinnamon

1 tablespoon unsalted butter, melted

⅔ cup (80 g) confectioners' sugar

3 tablespoons cornstarch

Directions

TO MAKE THE MARSHMALLOWS: Lightly coat a 9-inch/23 cm square pan with nonstick cooking spray. Place parchment on top, letting it overhang 2 sides, and then coat once more with nonstick cooking spray. (The first layer of nonstick spray will help to keep the parchment paper in place.)

Place the apple juice in a large bowl and sprinkle the gelatin over the surface; leave untouched to bloom.

In a medium saucepan, combine the granulated sugar, ½ cup water, and honey and cook, stirring, over medium heat until the sugar dissolves. Bring the mixture to a simmer and cook without stirring until a candy thermometer reads 240°F (116°C), 12 to 15 minutes.

Pour the sugar mixture into the gelatin mixture; use an electric mixer to beat on low speed until combined. Increase the speed to high and beat until thick and fluffy and the mixture triples in volume, about 10 minutes. Fold in all but 1 tablespoon of the freeze-dried apple crumbs (reserve those for the topping). Using a lightly oiled spatula, scrape the mixture into the prepared pan. Smooth out the top (the top surface will not be completely even). Set aside.

TO MAKE THE TOPPING: Place the flour, sugars, cinnamon, butter, and remaining tablespoon of freeze-dried apple crumbs in a bowl, tossing with a fork to combine. The topping is ready when it starts to come together into small crumbles. Sprinkle the topping on top of the marshmallow. Set aside in a cool place (not the refrigerator) for 8 hours or overnight to set.

In a small bowl, whisk together the confectioners' sugar and cornstarch. Lift the marshmallow from the pan and peel away the parchment paper. Lightly dust the top and bottom of the marshmallow with the confectioners' sugar mixture. Lightly coat a serrated knife with nonstick cooking spray and slice the marshmallow into 1-inch/2.5 cm cubes. Dust the cut sides with the confectioners' sugar mixture. The marshmallows will keep, layered between sheets of nonstick parchment, in an airtight container for 3 to 4 days.

217

GERMAN CHOCOLATE CARAMELS

These caramel candies are one of my husband's favorite treats. He will finish a handful before I'm even done wrapping a dozen of them. I totally get it: homemade caramels are so far superior to anything store-bought. He's also a smart man: He knows that because I love parceling these into tins and giving them as gifts, he needs to get his fix before they're gone.

MAKES 40 TO 50 CARAMELS

Nonstick cooking spray

2 cups (100 g) unsweetened dried coconut flakes

½ cup (65 g) pecans

¾ cup (150 g) granulated sugar

¾ cup (150 g) light brown sugar

1½ cups (375 ml) heavy whipping cream

6 tablespoons (84 g) unsalted butter

½ teaspoon salt

1 teaspoon pure vanilla extract

12 ounces (340 g) semisweet chocolate chips

Directions

Preheat the oven to 350°F (180°C). Line an 8-inch/20.5 cm square baking pan with parchment paper, leaving a 2-inch/5 cm overhang on 2 opposite sides. Spray the parchment paper with nonstick cooking spray.

Spread the coconut and pecans on a baking sheet and toast for 5 to 7 minutes, or until the coconut starts to turn lightly golden. Set aside.

In a deep saucepan, combine the sugars, cream, butter, and salt. Bring to a boil over medium heat and cook until golden brown, 2 to 4 minutes. Clip a candy thermometer to the side of the pan. Continue to cook the mixture, without stirring directly, using the handle of the pot to gently and carefully swirl the mixture. Cook over medium-low heat for 7 to 9 minutes, or until the thermometer reads 250°F (121°C), gently stirring occasionally to prevent the caramel from sticking to the sides of the saucepan.

Remove the pot from the heat and quickly add the vanilla, coconut, and pecans. Pour the mixture into the prepared baking dish and smooth out the top. Let cool at room temperature for 30 minutes before transferring the pan to the refrigerator to set for at least 2 hours.

Melt the chocolate in a microwave-safe bowl in a microwave on MEDIUM-HIGH in 30-second bursts, stirring between each burst.

Remove the caramel from the pan, using the parchment overhang to lift it, and place on a cutting board. Lightly coat the blade of a knife with nonstick cooking spray and cut the caramel into 1-inch/2.5 cm squares. Working with 1 at a time, using a fork, dip a caramel into the melted chocolate and evenly coat. Repeat with the remaining caramel squares. Refrigerate for 20 minutes, or until the chocolate hardens. Store in an airtight container for up to a week.

DARK CHOCOLATE and ESPRESSO BUTTERCRUNCH

Almond Roca was one of those teenage discoveries that changed my life. By life-changing, I mean it was for the teenage version of me. I spent a good few months of my lunch money forfeiting real midday sustenance for sweets with those little gold-wrapped bites. Nowadays, when I have that buttercrunch craving, I reach for my homemade version that I've punched up with crushed espresso beans.

MAKES ABOUT 1 POUND BUTTERCRUNCH

Nonstick cooking spray

2   tablespoons whole coffee beans

2   cups (450 g) unsalted butter

2   cups (400 g) granulated sugar

1   tablespoon light corn syrup

12 ounces (340 g) dark chocolate chips

2   cups (180 g) sliced almonds, toasted and chopped

Directions

Lightly coat a 13 x 9-inch/33 x 23 cm baking pan with nonstick cooking spray. Set aside.

Using a mortar and pestle, coarsely crush the whole coffee beans. Alternatively, place the beans in a plastic bag and crush with a rolling pin. Set aside.

In a large saucepan over medium-high heat, stir together the butter, sugar, corn syrup, and ¼ cup/59 ml of water and bring to a boil. Once boiling, stop stirring and continue to boil the mixture until it reaches 300°F (150°C) on a candy thermometer, about 20 minutes.

Turn off the heat and whisk in the crushed coffee beans. Working quickly, pour the mixture onto the prepared pan, tilting and turning the pan to spread the mixture to the pan's edges (the mixture may not completely reach the edges). Sprinkle the chocolate chips over the toffee and let stand for 1 to 2 minutes, then use an offset spatula to spread the chocolate evenly over the top. Sprinkle the almonds on top and press into the chocolate. Set the toffee aside to cool at room temperature, 1 to 2 hours, before breaking into shards.

LEMON and PISTACHIO TORRONE

This is one of those candies that never fails to impress those lucky enough to receive it. Once you see just how easy it is to make, you'll never eat or give the store-bought stuff again.

MAKES 40 (1½-INCH/4 CM) CANDY SQUARES

3   (11 x 8-inch/28 x 20.5 cm) wafer paper sheets (not spring roll wrappers) (optional)

Nonstick cooking spray, for pan (optional) and hands

1   cup (235 ml) honey

2½ cups (500 g) granulated sugar, divided

3   large egg whites

1   cup (120 g) roasted shelled pistachios, coarsely chopped

2   tablespoons lemon zest

All-purpose flour, for dusting

Directions

Arrange the wafer paper to fit the bottom of a 13 x 9-inch/33 x 23 cm quarter sheet pan, breaking off pieces of a second wafer sheet to fill any gaps. Alternatively, coat the pan with nonstick cooking spray, then cover with enough plastic wrap to leave a 1-inch/2.5 cm overhang.

In a medium saucepan over medium heat, bring the honey and 2 cups/400 g of the sugar to a simmer, stirring. Then, attach a candy thermometer to the side of the pan. Increase the heat and boil until the mixture reaches 315°F (157°C), 5 to 6 minutes.

In the meantime, in a large bowl, using an electric mixer on high speed, beat the egg whites and remaining ½ cup/100 g of sugar until stiff peaks form, 3 to 5 minutes; set aside.

Remove the honey mixture from the heat once the temperature is reached. Stir the mixture to help cool it to 300°F (150°C), about 2 minutes. Return to beating the egg whites on low speed, while slowly adding the honey mixture in a steady stream. Increase the speed to high and beat until the mixture triples in volume and is pale, stretchy, and begins to pull away from the sides of the bowl, about 10 minutes. Fold in the pistachios and lemon zest.

Turn out the nougat mixture onto a floured work surface and lightly coat your hands with nonstick cooking spray. Knead and fold the nougat back on itself a few times, or until it becomes pliable. Stretch and shape the nougat into the prepared pan. Top with a second sheet of wafer paper, using additional small pieces to completely cover the top, or plastic wrap. Press to an even finish with a rolling pin. Set aside to cool and set, about 4 hours or overnight.

Turn out the nougat onto a board and, using a large knife heated in running hot water (dry before using), cut into 1½-inch/4 cm squares, cleaning off and warming the knife as needed between cuts. Store the candy in an airtight container in the refrigerator.

CONFECTIONS

FUN FRUIT JELLIES

My little guy, Cole, is the fruitarian in the home, so when these come out on a tray, I know they won't last long. They go even faster if he's helping me make them, but I'll take it since I gain a kitchen assistant in the process.

MAKES ABOUT 60 (1-INCH/2.5 CM) PIECES

Nonstick cooking spray

1 cup (165 g) strawberries, hulled

1¼ cups (265 g) seedless strawberry jam

2 cups (400 g) granulated sugar, divided

1 tablespoon loose-leaf jasmine tea

3 envelopes unflavored powdered gelatin (2 tablespoons)

Directions

Lightly coat an 8-inch/20.5 cm square baking pan with nonstick cooking spray. Set aside.

Combine the strawberries, jam, and 1½ cups/300 g of the sugar in a blender and process until smooth. Measure out ½ cup/120 g of the mixture into a microwave-safe bowl and stir in ¾ cup/175 ml of cold water; set aside.

Transfer the remaining pureed fruit to a large saucepan, add the tea leaves, and bring to a boil over medium-high heat, about 5 minutes. Cook, stirring, until the mixture becomes thick and syrupy, about 2 minutes. Remove from the heat and set aside.

Sprinkle the gelatin over the reserved strawberry mixture. Set aside to let the gelatin bloom, about 3 minutes. Microwave the gelatin mixture on MEDIUM until it has a syruplike consistency, 15 to 20 seconds.

Stir the gelatin mixture into the cooked jasmine fruit. Strain the mixture through a fine-mesh sieve. Pour the mixture into the prepared pan. Transfer to the refrigerator and let set, 4 to 6 hours.

When ready to serve, unmold the jelly and cut into 1-inch/2.5 cm squares. Toss the cut jellies in remaining ½ cup/100 g of sugar to coat. Store in the fridge until ready to serve.

BRAMBILICIOUS MARSHMALLOWS

If you've never tried making your own marshmallows, then you're in for a treat. They are so much fluffier and cloudlike than any store-bought variety could ever be. Plus, they're the perfect canvas for infusing flavor. My favorite version takes both fresh blueberries and freeze-dried blueberries (which you can find at most health food stores, but don't worry if you need to skip it) to make a bright, tangy treat that's as yummy on its own as it is atop cakes or ice cream sundaes.

MAKES 36 MARSHMALLOWS

3   (¼-ounce) packets powdered gelatin

2   cups (400 g) granulated sugar

¼   cup (60 ml) honey

¼   teaspoon salt

½   cup (60 g) confectioners' sugar

3   tablespoons cornstarch

    Nonstick cooking spray

1   teaspoon vanilla bean paste

⅓   cup (34 g) dehydrated raspberries, ground to a powder

⅓   cup (34 g) dehydrated blueberries, ground to a powder

Directions

Place ½ cup/120 ml of water in a large bowl and sprinkle the gelatin over the top. Set aside to bloom.

In a medium saucepan, combine 3 tablespoons of water with the granulated sugar, honey, and salt. Cook and stir until the sugar dissolves. Bring the mixture to a simmer and cook, without stirring, until a candy thermometer reads 240°F (115°C), 8 to 10 minutes.

Remove the pan from the heat and slowly pour into a large bowl while beating with an electric mixer on low speed. Increase the speed to medium-high and beat for at least 10 minutes, until the mixture has nearly tripled in volume and the outside of the mixing bowl is no longer warm.

Sift together the confectioners' sugar and cornstarch. Prepare a 9-inch/23 cm square pan by lightly dusting it with nonstick cooking spray, then sifting in some of the confectioners' sugar mixture so that the entire inside of the pan is lightly coated. Tap out any excess, then set aside.

Once the marshmallow mixture is ready, add the vanilla bean paste and continue to beat for 30 seconds. Working quickly, remove about a third of the marshmallow mixture and randomly plop spoonfuls of it into the prepared pan. Fold the ground raspberries into the marshmallow mixture that remains in the bowl, then take about half of the mixture and plop it into the pan in spoonfuls, like the first third. Fold the ground blueberries into the remaining marshmallow mixture, and drop this mixture by the spoonful into the pan.

Use an offset spatula to lightly swirl the mixtures together throughout. Lightly sprinkle the top with the confectioners' sugar mixture (reserving the rest of the mixture), then cover and set on the counter to set completely, at least 4 hours and up to 8.

Lift the marshmallow from the pan and peel away the parchment paper. Lightly dust the top and bottom of the marshmallow with the confectioners' sugar mixture. Lightly coat a serrated knife with nonstick cooking spray and slice the marshmallow into 1-inch/2.5 cm cubes. Dust the cut sides with the confectioners' sugar mixture. The marshmallows will keep, layered between sheets of nonstick parchment, in an airtight container for 3 to 4 days.

COOL TREATS

Everybody (not just recipe hoarders like me!) needs a good stash of go-tos for those times when you don't want to fire up the oven or all that will do is something frosty. Whether you dive in headfirst with a Spumoni Ice Cream Cake or Caramel Crunch Latte Pops, or take baby steps with Honeydew Cucumber Margarita Pops or Toffee Ice Cream with Whiskey Caramel Ribbons, be sure to read through the recipe before you begin so you give your goodies enough time to "set up" in the fridge or freezer.

NEAPOLITAN PUDDING POPS

Neapolitan ice cream was always a childhood favorite of mine. I always thought it was like getting three desserts in one. When I started a family of my own, I passed that on to my boys who love this handheld version of a three-in-one treat.

MAKES 10 PUDDING POPS

3¼ cups (810 ml) whole milk

⅔ cup (140 g) granulated sugar

3 tablespoons cornstarch

¼ teaspoon salt

2 tablespoons ground dehydrated strawberries

1 tablespoon unsweetened cocoa powder

½ teaspoon vanilla bean paste

Directions

In a medium saucepan, whisk together the milk, sugar, cornstarch, and salt. Cook, whisking occasionally, over medium heat until the mixture starts to bubble, 3 to 5 minutes.

Divide the pudding evenly among 3 bowls. Add the ground strawberries to one bowl, the cocoa powder to the second bowl, and the vanilla bean paste to the third bowl.

Divide the vanilla pudding among the 10 molds, then the strawberry pudding, and finally the chocolate pudding. Place the lid, if you have one, on the pop mold, refrigerate for 1 hour to cool down before freezing (this makes a smoother consistency with the pudding pops), then insert a stick into each pudding pop and place in the freezer to freeze completely.

SPUMONI BROWNIE ICE CREAM CAKE

I couldn't include my Neapolitan Pudding Pops recipe (page 235) without including its sophisticated older sister, Spumoni Brownie Ice Cream Cake. This is one of those simple-as-simple-gets cake, perfect for the middle of summer when you don't want to fire up the oven. With just a few store-bought ingredients (namely, two flavors of ice cream—yes, please) and a couple turns of the wrist with a spatula, you have yourself a layered cake.

MAKES 6 TO 8 SERVINGS

For the cake

1   batch Chocolate Mousse Fudge Brownies (page 30), baked in a 9-inch (23 cm) round pan

Nonstick cooking spray

2   pints (946 ml) cherry ice cream, melted slightly

2   pints (946 ml) pistachio ice cream, melted slightly

For the topping

1   cup (250 ml) heavy whipping cream

¼   cup (50 g) granulated sugar

9   maraschino cherries

TO MAKE THE CAKE: Allow the brownie pan to cool completely on a wire rack, then freeze for 20 minutes to make cutting easier. Lightly coat a large serrated knife with nonstick cooking spray. Evenly cut the brownie into three horizontal layers.

Place 1 brownie layer onto the bottom of a 9-inch/23 cm round springform pan and spread with the softened cherry ice cream in an even layer, then top with a second brownie layer. Place plastic wrap over the top and freeze until firm, about 1 hour.

Remove the plastic wrap, spread with the pistachio ice cream in an even layer, then top with the remaining brownie layer. Place plastic wrap over the top and freeze until firm, about 1 hour.

WHEN READY TO SERVE, PREPARE THE TOPPING: Place a medium bowl in the freezer to chill for 10 minutes.

Remove the chilled bowl from the freezer. Combine the cream and sugar in the bowl and beat with an electric mixer on low speed until the mixture starts to thicken, 1 to 2 minutes. Increase the speed and beat until soft peaks form. Transfer the whipped cream to a pastry bag fitted with Wilton's 1M tip.

Gently remove the brownie cake from the pan and place on a serving platter. Pipe whipped cream around the perimeter of the top of the brownie and top the whipped cream with the maraschino cherries. Slice and serve immediately.

S'MORES ICE CREAM CAKE

What is better than an ice cream cake? One topped with toasted marshmallows. This is a party favorite that never fails to delight kids and adults alike.

MAKES 8 TO 10 SERVINGS

For the graham cracker crust

- ½ cup (113 g) unsalted butter
- 2 cups (200 g) graham cracker crumbs
- ¼ cup (55 g) lightly packed light brown sugar
- ¼ teaspoon salt

For the chocolate filling

- 2 quarts (1.9 L) chocolate ice cream
- 6 ounces (170 g) semisweet chocolate chips
- ¼ cup (60 ml) heavy whipping cream
- 1 tablespoon unsalted butter
- 1 tablespoon brown rice syrup
- ¼ teaspoon salt

For the marshmallow topping

- 3 large egg whites, at room temperature
- 1 cup (200 g) granulated sugar
- 1 teaspoon pure vanilla extract
- ¼ teaspoon salt

Directions

TO MAKE THE GRAHAM CRACKER CRUST: Melt half of the butter in a small saucepan over medium heat. Remove the pan from the heat and add the remaining butter; stir to melt. Add the graham cracker crumbs, brown sugar, and salt and mix until combined. Transfer the mixture to a 9-inch/23 cm round removable-bottom springform pan and press evenly on the bottom and up the sides. Transfer the pan to the freezer.

TO MAKE THE CHOCOLATE FILLING: Place the chocolate ice cream on the countertop to soften while you make the hot fudge swirl. Combine the chocolate chips, cream, butter, brown rice syrup, and salt in a microwave-safe dish. Microwave on HIGH in 30-second bursts, stirring well after each burst, until the mixture is melted and glossy. Set aside.

Place the softened ice cream in a large bowl and stir until it is of one consistency. Drizzle the hot fudge on top and stir gently until the ice cream is rippled with fudge. Quickly scrape the mixture into the graham cracker crust. Spread the ice cream to an even finish and place a piece of plastic wrap directly on the surface. Transfer the pan to the freezer to set completely, about 6 hours.

ONCE THE ICE CREAM IS SET, MAKE THE MARSHMALLOW TOPPING:
Combine the egg whites, sugar, vanilla, and salt in a large, heatproof bowl and place over a small saucepan of gently simmering water, making sure the water doesn't touch the bottom of the bowl. Whisk until the sugar dissolves and the mixture reaches 165°F (71°C). Remove the bowl from the heat. Using an electric mixer, beat the mixture on medium speed until it is frothy, then increase the speed to high and beat until stiff peaks form and the outside of the bowl is cool to the touch.

Top the ice cream cake with marshmallow topping. Using a kitchen torch, toast the marshmallow topping until golden brown. Remove the sides from the springform pan and serve immediately.

HONEYDEW CUCUMBER MARGARITA POPS

Of all the boozy pops I've featured on my blog, this continues to be the biggest hit. Honeydew and cucumbers are one of my favorite summer pairings—super fresh, a little sweet, a little floral, and a little herbaceous. Adding some tequila and triple sec makes this the perfect adult poolside treat.

MAKES 8 TO 10 POPS

1   (1 pound/455 g) honeydew melon, skin and seeds removed

1   (10-ounce/285 g) cucumber, peeled

4   ounces (120 ml) tequila

1   tablespoon triple sec

1   tablespoon freshly squeezed lime juice

1   tablespoon mint syrup

3   large sprigs mint

Directions

In a blender or food processor, combine all the ingredients and blend until completely smooth.

Divide the mixture equally among eight to ten 2-ounce/60 ml ice pop molds and freeze for 1 hour. Cover the mold with a layer of foil and cut a tiny hole through the foil in the center of each well. Insert a Popsicle stick into each hole. Continue to freeze the pops for 4 to 6 hours. To release the pops, run hot water over the outside of the mold for 2 to 3 seconds. Pop out and serve.

GRILLED DONUT PB&J ICE CREAM SANDWICHES

I love taking a standby favorite and mashing it up against another favorite—like the PB&J + donut. If there was ever a dessert that made me a hero, this is it. My boys went absolutely crazy for this at first bite—so much so that if we are short on time and patience, we'll cheat the homemade ice cream version and use high-quality store-bought vanilla ice cream and stir in ¼ cup of peanut butter to every cup of vanilla ice cream.

MAKES 4 ICE CREAM SANDWICHES

For the ice cream

6   large egg yolks

½   cup (100 g) granulated sugar

2   teaspoons pure vanilla extract

1   cup (240 ml) heavy whipping cream, softly whipped

½   cup (135 g) creamy peanut butter

For assembly

Nonstick cooking spray

4   glazed donuts

1   cup (210 g) strawberry jam

Directions

TO MAKE THE ICE CREAM: Prepare an ice bath by placing ice in a large bowl (making sure it's large enough to accommodate the bowl of custard, below), so it's half-full with ice. Pour ¼ cup/60 ml of cold water over the ice. Set aside.

Place a heatproof bowl over a pot of boiling water so it doesn't touch the water, and whisk together the egg yolks and sugar in the bowl until well combined. Continue to cook, stirring, until a custard forms on a spoon and a clearly drawn line through it can hold its shape, or until the temperature reaches 165°F (74°C) on a candy thermometer, 10 to 12 minutes. Take great care not to overcook.

Remove the bowl from the heat and place in the ice bath. Gently stir in the vanilla, then stir the mixture about every 5 minutes to help cool it to room temperature (it may lose some volume; this is normal). Once the mixture is at room temperature, fold in the whipped cream and peanut butter.

Scrape the mixture into a 9 x 5-inch/ 23 x 12.5 cm loaf pan. Cover and freeze until set, about 8 hours.

Heat a grill to medium. Lightly coat the grates with nonstick cooking spray. Grill the donuts until they have good grill marks, about 2 minutes. Flip and grill the opposite side. Remove from the grill and allow to cool for 5 minutes.

TO ASSEMBLE: Cut the grilled donuts in half horizontally and place 1 or 2 scoops of ice cream on a donut half. Spread jam onto a second donut half and place on top of the ice cream. Repeat to form the other sandwiches. Serve immediately.

CARAMEL CRUNCH LATTE POPS

These pops always transport me back to my childhood, when I had my first taste of coffee ice cream. I remember the pints in the freezer were reserved for my dad. Like most kids, I wasn't allowed to have coffee in any form, but I was naturally curious, always wanting what I couldn't have, and I would sneak little spoonfuls of it. These pops remind me of those stolen creamy bites of coffee, but now I have to hide these bites from our kids.

MAKES 10 POPS

1 pint (453 g) vanilla ice cream, softened

3 tablespoons finely chopped chocolate-covered coffee beans, divided

¼ cup (60 ml) brewed espresso, cooled to room temperature

¼ cup (60 ml) whole milk

⅓ cup (80 ml) caramel sauce (home-made, page 255 [omit whiskey], or store-bought), divided

For the chocolate coating

8 ounces (250 g) dark chocolate (65% cacao or more), finely chopped

1 cup (210 g) refined coconut oil

¼ cup (90 g) light corn syrup

Directions

In a large bowl, fold together the ice cream and crushed coffee beans. Fold in the espresso, milk, and caramel sauce.

Pour the mixture into 10 Popsicle molds. Freeze for at least 6 hours.

TO MAKE THE CHOCOLATE COATING: In a microwave-safe bowl, stir together the chocolate, coconut oil, and corn syrup. Microwave in 7- to 10-second bursts on MEDIUM until the mixture is smooth and well combined, making sure to stir between bursts. Alternatively, melt in a small saucepan over very low heat until everything is smooth and combined, stirring constantly. Pour the mixture into a narrow glass that will accommodate a pop. Line a baking sheet with parchment paper.

To finish, remove the pops from the freezer. To release the pops, run hot water over the outside of the mold for 2 to 3 seconds. Working with 1 pop at a time, dip the pop into the chocolate coating, or alternately, drizzle chocolate coating on top. Transfer to the prepared baking sheet. Sprinkle with the remaining crushed coffee beans. Repeat with the remaining pops. Return the pops to the freezer until ready to eat.

BERRY BLAST SMOOTHIE POPS

I don't usually like to eat on the go, but when I do, I'll take it in pop form and with a little side of healthy to go with it. I keep my freezer well stocked with these for the boys, especially since this is much easier to eat in the car than a smoothie bowl.

MAKES 10 POPS

4 ounces (113 g) strawberries

4 ounces (113 g) raspberries

4 ounces (113 g) blueberries

4 to 5 tablespoons granulated sugar

4 cups (907 g) vanilla Greek yogurt

¼ cup (59 ml) milk

¼ cup (59 ml) honey

4 ounces (115 g) granola

Directions ....

Combine the strawberries and raspberries in a medium pan over medium-high heat and cook until the mixture simmers rapidly. Cook for 10 to 12 minutes, stirring often, until the mixture thickens. Remove from the heat, pour into a heat-safe bowl, and let cool to room temperature. Clean the pot and repeat the cooking process with the blueberries. (If the berries need some sweetening, add 4 to 5 tablespoons of the sugar to achieve your preferred sweetness.)

In a large bowl, mix together the yogurt, milk, and honey. The mixture will be thick but pourable.

TO ASSEMBLE: Pour a tablespoon or two of yogurt into each of 10 Popsicle molds. Add a tablespoon of granola and then a tablespoon or two of cooked fruit. Continue layering, alternating the strawberry–raspberry and blueberry layers until the molds are filled. Tap each mold against the counter to release any air bubbles. Insert a Popsicle stick and freeze for at least 6 hours (the time will vary according to your freezer's setting and how full it is). To remove the smoothie pops from a mold, run hot water around the outside of the pop mold. Wrap each frozen pop in parchment paper and store in a sealed plastic bag in the freezer. The pops will keep for up to 3 weeks.

CHOCOLATE MINT CHIP ICE CREAM SANDWICHES

If you are a fan of mint chip ice cream, then this is the ice cream sandwich for you. Sure, you can punch up the mint flavor with a little peppermint extract, but I prefer the subtlety of real mint leaves steeped in the cream, and then elevating the mint.

MAKES 2 DOZEN 2-INCH/5 CM SQUARE SANDWICHES

1   cup (250 ml) milk

2   cups (500 ml) heavy whipping cream

Leaves from 1 large bunch mint

6   large egg yolks

¾   cup (150 g) granulated sugar

1   tablespoon pure vanilla extract

6   ounces (170 g) bittersweet chocolate, finely chopped

24 chocolate wafer cookies

In a saucepan over medium heat, heat the milk and cream to a simmer, 3 to 4 minutes. Remove from the heat. Add the mint leaves, cover, allow to cool to room temperature, then allow to steep in the refrigerator for 2 hours. Strain the mixture and discard the mint leaves.

Prepare an ice bath by placing ice in a large bowl (making sure it's large enough to accommodate the bowl you will use in the following step) so it's half-full with ice. Pour ¼ cup/60 ml of cold water over the ice. Set aside.

Gently reheat the cream mixture until warm; set aside. Set a heatproof bowl over a pot of boiling water, and whisk together the egg yolks and sugar in the bowl until well combined. Gradually pour the warmed cream mixture into the yolk mixture, whisking constantly. Continue to cook, stirring, until a custard forms on a spoon and a clearly drawn line through it can hold its shape, or until the temperature reaches 165°F (74°C) on a candy thermometer, 10 to 12 minutes. Take great care not to overcook.

Remove the bowl from the heat and place in the ice bath. Gently stir in the vanilla, then stir the mixture about every 5 minutes to help cool it to room temperature (it may lose some volume; this is normal). Once the mixture is at room temperature, fold in the chopped chocolate.

Scrape the ice cream mixture into a 9 x 5-inch/23 x 12.5 cm loaf pan. Cover and freeze until set, about 8 hours.

To assemble, place a scoop of ice cream on 1 chocolate wafer cookie and place a second cookie on top. Serve right away, or return the sandwiches to the freezer until ready to serve.

TOFFEE ICE CREAM *with* WHISKEY CARAMEL RIBBONS

Next to flavor, I'm all about texture, so when I had the idea to make a whiskey caramel-laced ice cream, I knew it needed a crunchy toffee bite to play against the cold creaminess of the ice cream. You can of course use store-bought toffee, or you can go ahead and make the buttercrunch toffee from page 220. If you decide to go straight homemade, leave the crushed espresso beans in it as it will give this ice cream an added layer of flavor.

MAKES 1½ PINTS/710 ML ICE CREAM

For the whiskey caramel sauce

- 1 cup (200 g) granulated sugar
- ½ cup (120 ml) heavy whipping cream
- 2 tablespoons unsalted butter
- ¼ cup (60 ml) whiskey
  Pinch of sea salt

For the ice cream base

- 2 cups (500 ml) heavy whipping cream, divided
- 3 whole vanilla beans
  Nonstick cooking spray
- 6 large egg yolks, at room temperature
- 1 large egg, at room temperature
- ½ cup (100 g) granulated sugar
- ½ teaspoon kosher salt
- 1 tablespoon vanilla bean paste

- 1 pound (455 g) English toffee (store-bought or homemade, page 220)

TO MAKE THE WHISKEY CARAMEL SAUCE: Place the sugar and ¼ cup/60 ml of water in a small saucepan. Cook, stirring, over medium-high heat until the sugar is dissolved, using a pastry brush to wash down any sugar crystals from the sides of the pot. Bring to a boil, about 3 minutes. Once boiling, do not stir directly. Instead, holding the long handle of the pot, tilt and swirl the mixture to distribute the heat evenly. At 7 to 8 minutes, the color will start to change. Watch the mixture closely and continue to tilt and swirl the pan to even out the color. Continue to cook and swirl until the mixture is a dark amber, 1 to 2 minutes once the first shade of color starts to appear. Remove from the heat immediately. Add the cream carefully, as it will bubble and splatter. Add the butter and stir until fully dissolved. Stir in the whiskey and salt. The caramel can be made 1 week ahead and kept covered and refrigerated.

TO MAKE THE ICE CREAM BASE: Place 1 cup/250 ml of the cream in a large pot. Halve the vanilla beans lengthwise. Scrape the seeds into the cream and stir in the pods. Bring the mixture to a boil over medium-high heat. Remove the pan from the heat and let stand for 10 minutes. Stir in the remaining cup/250 ml of cream and allow the mixture to cool to room temperature. Chill the mixture in the refrigerator for at least 2 hours or overnight.

Lightly grease a 9 x 5-inch/23 x 12.5 cm loaf pan with nonstick cooking spray (this will prevent the plastic wrap from shifting around in the pan). Line the pan with plastic wrap, leaving a 4-inch overhang on each side. Set aside.

(directions continue)

Fill a medium saucepan with water and bring to a simmer over medium heat. Whisk together the egg yolks, egg, sugar, and salt in a large bowl. Set the bowl over the simmering water, making sure the bottom does not touch the water. Attach a thermometer to the side of the bowl. Whisk the mixture continuously until it reaches 175°F (79°C). Using an electric mixer on medium-high speed, beat until the mixture doubles in volume and is cool to the touch, about 7 minutes. Add the vanilla paste and beat until well combined. Set aside and clean the beaters.

Remove the chilled cream mixture from the refrigerator and beat on high speed with clean beaters until soft peaks form. Add half of the whipped cream to the whipped egg mixture and fold until just streaky. Fold in the crumbled toffee. Pour one third of mixture into the prepared pan and drizzle the whiskey caramel on top; repeat the layering two more times. Drag a knife through the ice cream mixture for a rippled ribbon effect. Cover and freeze for at least 8 hours or overnight.

Index

Note: Page references in *italics* indicate photographs.

E

Earl Grey
  and Orange Shortbread Cookies, Chocolate-
    Dipped, 55–57, *56*
  Cream and Strawberry Tart, 80–82, *81*
  London Fog Blueberry Hand Pies, 94–96, *95*
Éclairs, Raspberry, with Vanilla Bean Cream,
    188–191, *189*

F

Fluffernutter Tart, 83–85, *84*
Fruit. *See also* Berry(ies); *specific fruits*
  and Nut Matzo Brittle, 204–206, *205*
  Jellies, Fun, 226–227
Fudge, Mocha Crunch, *202,* 203
Funnel Cake Bites, Cinnamon and Sugar, 192–193
Funnel Cake Cupcakes, 129–131, *130*

G

German Chocolate Caramels, 218–219
Graham crackers and crumbs
  Campfire Granola Bars, 41–43, *42*
  Fluffernutter Tart, 83–85, *84*
  Graham Dutch Apple Pie, 72–74, *73*
  Lemon Ricotta Cheesecake with Fresh
    Berries, 70–71
  S'mores Ice Cream Cake, 239–241
Granola
  Apple Pecan, 24–26, *25*
  Bars, Campfire, 41–43, *42*
Grapefruit and Vanilla Bean Panna Cotta Tart,
    75–76

H

Hand Pies, London Fog Blueberry, 94–96, *95*
Honeydew Cucumber Margarita Pops, *242,* 243
Honey Grilled Peaches with Whipped Ricotta,
    170–172, *171*

I

Ice Cream
  Cake, S'mores, 239–241
  Cake, Spumoni Brownie, 236–238, *237*
  Caramel Crunch Latte Pops, 247–249, *248*

Chocolate Mint Chip, Sandwiches, 252–254,
    253
  Sandwiches, Grilled Donut PB&J, 244–246,
    245
  Toffee, with Whiskey Caramel Ribbons,
    255–258, *256*

J

Jellies, Fun Fruit, 226–227

L

Lamingtons, Strawberry and Cream, 179–181
Lemon
  and Pistachio Torrone, 223–225, *224*
  Marshmallow Pie Pops, *158,* 159–160
  Poppy Seed Smashed Berry Bundt Cake,
    116–118, *117*
  Raspberry Lemonade Cupcakes, 151–153, *152*
  Ricotta Cheesecake with Fresh Berries, 70–71
Lime
  Blackberry Jam and Honey Whipped Cream,
    Black Tea Cake with, 147–150, *148*
  Sour Cherry Pie, 89–90

M

Maple Pecan Frosting, Banana Cupcakes with,
    122–124, *123*
Margarita Pops, Honeydew Cucumber, *242,* 243
Marshmallow(s)
  Apple Pie, 215–217, *216*
  Brambilicious, 228–230, *229*
  Campfire Granola Bars, 41–43, *42*
  Lemon Pie Pops, *158,* 159–160
  Mocha Crunch Fudge, *202,* 203
  Roasted, and Hot Chocolate Pots de Creme,
    194–197, *195*
  Rocky Road Cookies, 21–23, *22*
  S'mores Ice Cream Cake, 239–241
Matzo Brittle, Fruit and Nut, 204–206, *205*
Meringue Kisses, Rainbow Rippled, 213–214
Mint Chocolate Chip Ice Cream Sandwiches,
    252–254, *253*
Mississippi Mud Pie, 91–93, *92*
Mocha Crunch Fudge, *202,* 203
Molasses Bundt Cake with Bourbon Caramel
    Sauce, 132–134, *133*

BAKER'S ROYALE

263